Living Feng Shui
Personal Stories

Carole J. Hyder

THE CROSSING PRESS
FREEDOM, CALIFORNIA

For information on bulk purchases or group discounts for this and other Crossing Press titles, please contact our Special Sales Manager at 800/777-1048.

Visit our Web site: www.crossingpress.com

Library of Congress Cataloging-in-Publication Data

Hyder, Carole J.
  Living feng shui : personal stories / Carole J. Hyder.
    p. cm.
  ISBN 1-58091-115-3
  1. Feng shui.   I. Title.
  BF1779.F4 H96 2001
  133.3'337--dc21

                          2001037129

              0   9   8   7   6   5   4   3   2   1

Acknowledgments

There are many people to whom I'd like to extend gratitude. This book, and my first one, would never have seen the light of day had it not been for Professor Thomas Lin Yun. A Buddhist teacher, he blends our Western mind-set with the traditional principles of Feng Shui. Only through his efforts, his insights, and his wisdom are we able to take advantage of this information and put it to work.

My subsequent studies with Roger Green of Australia have succeeded in deepening my understanding of the power and subtleties of Feng Shui.

I owe a huge thank you to my readers who pored over the manuscript endlessly: Suzi Michael, Janet Sawyer, Jeanie Pullen, Rita Roque, Deb O'Donnell.

As usual, my designer Dorie McClelland infused the stories with her magic. Thanks to her, the book looks the way it does. She so remarkably orchestrates the energy around my ideas that we end up with a final product of unsurpassed beauty and exquisite design. But then I expect nothing less from her.

My dear husband Tom unselfishly lent his time and energy to this endeavor. Uncomplainingly, he read and re-read the stories before they ever got to the actual readers. A lifetime of gratitude is due him for being my support, my friend, and for living Feng Shui with me.

I dedicate this book to all the people who have so generously taught me and continue to teach me about living Feng Shui.

Contents

Foreword

Professor Thomas Lin Yun

The Chinese have an ancient proverb: "It is better to be happy with a crowd than to be happy alone." After I read Carole Hyder's new book, I thought about her. When she attended my workshops she was totally devoted to her work so that "the indigo ink is bluer than the indigo plant from which it comes."* To put it simply, when Carole studied Feng Shui, she did it wholeheartedly and with diligence. After she acquired the necessary skills, she was then able to help those people who needed Feng Shui adjustment. Finally, she carefully made records of case studies and made an accurate and honest account of the truth before and after Black Sect Tantric Buddhist Feng Shui adjustment.

Carole then had an in-depth understanding of the power of Black Sect Tantric Buddhist Feng Shui perspective. Her abilities and her success allowed her to have an indescribable happiness and comfort that stemmed from deep in her heart. Carole has turned this emotional happiness into words and wrote this great book that is very clear and easy to understand. It will allow her clients, beneficiaries, relatives, and friends, and those readers who don't understand Feng Shui, to acquire an immediate resonance. This is why I said that Carole exalted the spirit and love of "it is better to be happy with a crowd than to be happy alone."

Every chapter uses actual case studies. Every case study is made clearer with illustrations of the floor plan, and contrasts the space before and after a Feng Shui adjustment. If it were possible to reveal the actual year, month, date, hour, and the area where these houses, apartments, and office buildings were located, it would enable the reader to understand even more clearly that this is absolute truth being chronicled. Even though this book does not introduce Feng Shui through theory, logic, or historical lineage, these case studies allow the reader to cross all barriers and immediately immerse himself in the phenomenon of Feng Shui. This kind of experience is much more advanced and direct than traditional teaching methods.

The narration of a good book does not rely on clear penmanship or rich content. There should also be good writing, careful arrangement, love, and inspiration. Some books are written well, but the content is too profound to be understood. Some books have smooth penmanship, but the content is rather empty. Some books are well written and have good content, but the effect of the writing skills is lost because there is no understanding of the readers' needs. Carole's new book is carefully designed so that is has all of the above stated advantages and none of the above stated shortcomings. This is another special value that sets it apart from other publications. I have strong faith that the readers will share my feelings.

---

*This is a proverb that means that the student is so diligent that his achievements surpass that of his teacher. It is often used by teachers to show their humility— *Translated from Chinese by Mary R. Hsu*

See the blessings of Professor Thomas Lin Yun on pages 265–277.

Introduction

In 1998, I wrote a little book called *Wind and Water: Your Personal Feng Shui Journey.* The response was overwhelming. I heard from people all over the world about how the book impacted them. Its format was simple, comprised of page-long Feng Shui suggestions and recommendations. A reader could integrate the book page by page, or issue by issue. Or they could begin on page one and read straight through to the end. Whichever way they did it, people were touched.

I continued my work as a Feng Shui consultant, teaching and meeting people, and studying more about Feng Shui. I had the privilege of working very intimately with many open and heart-centered individuals. As a result, I birthed another book. My intention was to provide real-life case studies of how people are living in their spaces.

The names have been changed for obvious reasons. But the situations and the results are true. I have included my working drawings, which are not intended to be architectural renderings or blueprints, but are integral to the specific stories.

I am blessed to have Feng Shui in my life, not only for what it has done for me, but for the opportunities to work so intimately and deeply with others, to see the changes they have put in place, and to celebrate with them.

Feng Shui can give you a new perspective for looking at the space where you work and where you live. One of the basic principles of Feng Shui is that your space mirrors your life. It follows that you will get a new perspective on your life by using Feng Shui tools. They can provide ways to create a space that will bring about prosperity, productivity, partners, and peace. By incorporating some of the simplest and smallest suggestions, it is not hard to realize the power of Feng Shui.

In most cases, the adjustments for Feng Shui are subtle and affordable. Sometimes the adjustment is not even visible, such as placing a small mirror behind a painting or in a closet, or placing coins in the foundation of a new building. The power of the adjustment does not depend on the object as much as the intention with which the object is placed. The stronger the intent, the more dramatic the results.

Analyzing a space

There are three ways in which to analyze a space according to Feng Shui. One way is to assess the shape of the building, the house, or a room. It is ideal to have a simple and uncomplicated system of walls that holds your life together. The more structural angles and complications in a space, the more activity the occupants' lives will take on. Less is more.

Another way is to look at what you own, how much you own, and where you put it. In considering this, it may be necessary for you to deal with some clutter issues. In Feng Shui, everything is energy. The more possessions you have, the more energy is required to maintain them or keep them. Sometimes changing the position of a sofa and chairs can create a more conversational arrangement, opening up lines of communication between family members. Sometimes changing the location of the bed can enable someone to sleep better. Sometimes de-cluttering a countertop or a desk can open up new channels to creativity and clear thinking. Again, less is more.

Finally, you can check out the layout of a space based on a mental map called a *bagua*, to determine the placement of nine life issues. When a bagua is appropriately placed and enhanced, your life begins to manifest good fortune and blessed occurrences. The nine areas of the bagua are shown on the next page.

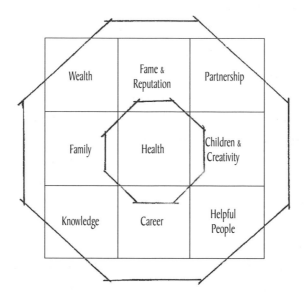

Wealth	Fame & Reputation	Partnership
Family	Health	Children & Creativity
Knowledge	Career	Helpful People

The front door

You can place this mental map over the main floor of a building or a home, an individual room, even a desktop. The orientation of the bagua is determined by the position of the front door. The front door, however, may not be the door you use all of the time. Nevertheless, the entrance that was architecturally intended to be the front door is the one with which you will work. The front entrance is always in the Knowledge, Career, or Helpful People area.

If you look at your space as though flying above it, include in the bagua anything that has a roof and sides. Therefore, include an attached garage or a screened-in porch in the layout. A deck and overhangs are not part of the bagua because they do not have both a roof and sides.

After incorporating all the pieces that need to be considered, divide your space into three equal areas left to right, and three equal areas front to back. Each area matches one of those shown on the bagua diagram. From the perspective of the street, if your front door is to the left on the house, you have a Knowledge door. If your front door is in the center, you have a Career door. Likewise, if your door is located more to the right, you have a Helpful People door. The Wealth area is in the back-left corner of your space. The Partnership area is in the back right corner, and the Health is in the center.

Laying the bagua over a house

As you first begin to work with the bagua, do not concern yourself with the interior walls. Be most concerned with mapping out the

Knowledge door   Career door   Helpful People door

different areas on the overall layout. Once the nine areas have been determined, you can then observe where the interior walls are located. The examples on the following two pages show how the bagua is superimposed over a house.

ENTRY

The bagua superimposed over a house

ENTRY

The bagua superimposed over a house

Missing pieces and extensions

You will probably realize that your house is not a perfect square or rectangle. In all likelihood, it will have some pieces protruding and some missing. When a piece is missing, it indicates a depletion or challenge in that bagua area. You want to "capture" missing areas by planting a tree in the corner, installing a flagpole or light post, positioning a fountain or birdbath, running a fence around the area, or creating any marker that will reinforce your intention to complete what is missing.

If you have little pieces protruding from the main part of your house, you have an extension in the corresponding area of the bagua. An extension is auspicious and gives you extra energy in that particular area. Extensions do not need to be changed or adjusted. See the examples on the following page.

Missing piece in Partnership

Missing piece in Career

Extension in Wealth

Extension in Children and Creativity

Individual rooms

There are times when it is difficult to determine which way the bagua lays out. For example, you may have a door that doesn't face the street or a slanted door. Then you incorporate the Feng Shui bagua on a room-by-room basis. When you lay out a bagua over an individual room, determine the front entry to the room. If you have more than one entrance into a room, the front entry is the one used most frequently or the one closest to the main front door. The bagua areas of an individual room could be in a different orientation than the bagua of the main floor. It is not important that they match. You can also superimpose the bagua over your desk and your bed. See the example on the following page.

The bagua superimposed over individual rooms in different orientations.
The "H" designates the Health area.
The "W" designates the Wealth area.
The "P" designates the Partnership area.

Color

Each area of the bagua is not only represented by a life issue but also by a color. The color, or its variation, can be used in the corresponding part of the bagua. For example, if Wealth is a problem, you can integrate something purple, lavender, magenta, or mauve in that area. Because colors are so personal, it is very important that you use a color you love, otherwise don't use the color at all. See baguas on the following pages.

Explanation of the areas of the bagua

Career

A career is a direction to use your abilities, talents, and interests. A career takes you from one phase of your life to the next. It is a vehicle for your passion, even if you don't get paid for it. Many people find enjoyment in their paying professions, yet they also love to volunteer, garden, or paint. All of these are activities and directions for your pursuits and are classified under the Career area of the bagua.

Knowledge

The area of Knowledge is about learning and education in whatever form that may take for you—a high school diploma, a graduate degree,

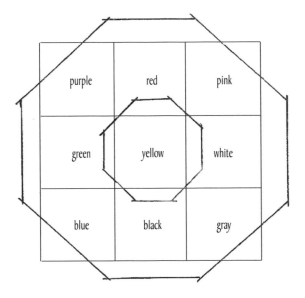

purple | red | pink

green | yellow | white

blue | black | gray

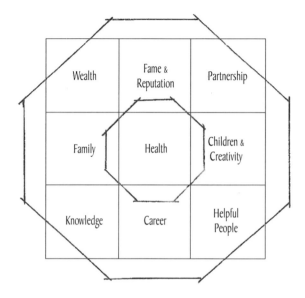

Wealth	Fame & Reputation	Partnership
Family	Health	Children & Creativity
Knowledge	Career	Helpful People

a certification or license in a field of interest, or simply reading up on a topic. It can also be about your children's educational issues. It further reflects the ascent to higher self-knowledge, learning about yourself. It also reflects the undertaking to share your knowledge or information with others.

Family
Family issues include your family of origin such as parents, siblings, cousins, and relations. It also includes anyone you consider your extended family, such as good friends, neighbors, and colleagues. This area is most commonly recognized as dealing with your roots and where you came from. It also reflects groups brought together for a specific purpose, such as work teams, church groups, or committees.

Wealth
Wealth is about your money coming in and going out. How you get your money (wages, lottery, inheritance, stocks, gifts, funding) balances how you spend your money (expenses, gifts, charity, inheritance, retirement).

Fame and Reputation

The Fame and Reputation area stands for your image and how the world sees you. It represents your good name and your standing in the community. In a business setting, it reflects your connection to the outside world and community, and your reputation.

Partnership

The Partnership area represents personal partners, business partners, spiritual partners, and partnering with yourself. Getting to know yourself and working through some issues with a partner fall into this category.

Children and Creativity

Children and Creativity stands for your own children and other children you may be involved with. It also may stand for your inner child. It includes anything which you may "birth" in your life in addition to children—a book, a thesis, poetry, music, your stories.

Helpful People

Helpful People are often referred to as angels, particularly when they show up unexpectedly with exactly what you need when you need it. Helpful people are those who support you emotionally and sometimes financially. They can be a best friend, a relative, a minister, a plumber. A helpful person can be a real estate agent who helps you sell your house or a travel agent who gets you from here to there. A helpful person can be a client for your business. As part of the ebb and flow of Feng Shui, being a helpful person is as important as having helpful people or benefactors in your life. Sometimes you need to be one before you will see any benefactors in your own life.

Health

The center of the bagua is the Health area. This area represents health on physical, mental, emotional, and spiritual levels. It is the hub or core around which everything else revolves. It follows that if you are not feeling well, you do not do your job well; you do not relate to your partner or children in a patient, loving manner; your productivity and creativity are affected; your pay may even be affected. Feeling well can support functioning well.

Stories

De-cluttering for a New Life

When I first met Ned, he didn't know much about Feng Shui other than what he had read in a magazine, but he thought it would be interesting to set up an appointment. Besides, he was in a desperate state which required equally desperate measures.

On my way to his home, three things happened to give me a hint as to what lay ahead. First, a big truck had stalled in the middle of a street a few blocks from my home as it was making a left-hand turn. Traffic was backed up for several blocks in both directions as cars slowly took turns getting around this obstacle. Second, when I finally got on the freeway, the ramp I was intending to take to Ned's town was under construction, and I had to make a quick adjustment as to how I was going to get there. Finally, despite his clear directions, I was unable to locate his house. As I drove around trying to get my bearings, I knew something unusual was going to happen.

Finally, I got there and everything looked fine until the door opened. He was living in the upper part of a duplex with tenants below him. It was apparent that the tenants were enjoying some loud rap music. The bass from their stereo made it seem as if Ned's space had a pulse. He ran down the stairs to plead with them to turn the sound down. He told me later that he was embroiled in a severe battle trying to evict them.

As Ned ran downstairs, I had a chance to look around. It looked as though he had just moved in. There were boxes, bags, and piles of stuff stacked everywhere. Anything resembling a table was full of stuff, and there seemed to be no place to enjoy a meal. I found a narrow pathway to a bedroom where evidently Ned slept. I remained standing until he returned because there was simply no place to sit down.

Ned's story was pretty simple. Three to four years ago he divorced a woman for whom he clearly had strong feelings, moved away from the pain of it all, took a production job, bought a duplex, and lost sight of his dreams. He was not well, obviously smoked, and was not very happy. He looked to me for some clue about where to begin to sort out his life. I tried to get him to talk about what he wanted, any goals he had, where he saw himself in a year or two. But these questions he couldn't even consider. All he wanted was immediate relief. The stalled semi, the closed ramp, and getting lost—everything began to make sense to me.

When I'm in an overwhelming situation, the best plan is to do the simplest thing. I knew he couldn't take on an immense Feng Shui project. Besides, I could sense that he was feeling ashamed about the condition of his space now that I was standing in it. Yet, I had to believe he was ready for something to happen or he wouldn't have called me. We had a brief introductory talk about Feng Shui, what it is, where it comes from, and the importance of energy and intention. Ned followed me pretty closely. I suggested that we have a short initial appointment to give him time to implement a few small things and then I'd come back to consider his next step.

He seemed okay with this idea—relieved actually. As a first remedy he could easily do, I suggested he hang a round, faceted crystal in the center of his space *(see Original Plan)* to calm and balance the space and to begin a gentle, subtle movement of the energy (●). Once the energy would start to shift, he would be more inclined to get himself unstuck and therefore deal with his clutter. We spent a few minutes measuring out his space to determine where the exact center was located. He said he would get the crystal the next time he was near a store.

That seemed simple enough. My next suggestion was to consider moving his bedroom. He currently was sleeping in the front of his

KITCHEN

BDRM.

DINING RM.

ENTRY

LIVING RM.

BDRM.

Original Plan

house and was quick to tell me that he didn't sleep well—some nights not at all. I suggested that he take the room near the back of his apartment where it would be quieter and feel safer. It was a smaller room, but I was sure the advantages would outweigh the disadvantage. He began to object. He didn't want to move all the stuff from one room to another, but I reminded him that all I wanted him to move was his bed and dresser. The books, computer, treadmill, boxes of miscellaneous things, his gun collection, and a television were not to be moved into his new room.

And, of course, he needed to remove all the things he presently had in that back room. I suggested that, as a symbol of a new start, he might want to clean the window there, shampoo the carpet, and maybe paint the walls before moving his bed in. He didn't seem too daunted by this switch—puzzled maybe, but not daunted. Besides, all the stuff in the back room would blend nicely with all the other things stacked around! That was all I wanted him to do for now. We rescheduled another appointment a month later.

Although open to the idea of energy and its potential impact on someone, Ned was relatively new to the concept of working with the environment. But Feng Shui sounded like the solution to his problem of feeling overwhelmed, tired, confused, and in need of direction.

I returned to Ned's home a month later. Ned immediately showed me the crystal he had hung in the center of the house. He wasn't sure he had done it right and explained in great detail how hard it was to find a crystal and how long it took to find the right little nail from which to hang it. But he seemed quite proud of his accomplishment.

He was anxious to show me his new bedroom *(see Final Plan)*. I noticed on my way to the back of the house that the clutter was still there, and the boxes and bags hadn't been moved. Nevertheless, Ned had managed to clear the back bedroom and had moved his bed into the back corner furthest from the door (the command position). He had moved one dresser in there as well. When he started to clean the carpet, he realized that it wasn't tacked down very securely and he could see a beautiful, pristine hardwood floor underneath. So he removed the carpet. The walls had a lovely coat of green paint and the window was sparkling clean. He showed me how easily it opened up now, where before it had been stuck. Repairing anything broken or malfunctioning supports a smoother, less aggravating life. Ned seemed

KITCHEN

BDRM.

DINING ROOM

ENTRY

LIVING ROOM

OFFICE

Final Plan

tentatively proud of his accomplishment, but was not sure if he had done everything right. However, he did admit he was sleeping a little better in this room. Of course, he was quick to add that the tenant's stereo was no longer directly under his bedroom so naturally it would be quieter. I let it go at that.

I made a couple of additional suggestions for the bedroom—he could bring in a chair so he could sit by the window. I also recommended that he move his bed away from the wall so he could get in and out of bed on either side. Ned didn't think more would be practical, but changed his mind. He was willing to consider leaving it out in the room when I explained the importance of having options in life—even when getting in and out of bed.

The next area of concern was where he ate his meals. He made it clear that my question was stupid since the kitchen table was buried with stuff as were the chairs. He ate on a recliner in the living room in front of the television. I explained that whether he ate there or not, he still needed to have a special place designated for eating. He realized that meant cleaning off the kitchen table. I encouraged him not just to move the stuff to another part of the house, but to make some decisions whether to keep it or not. He reluctantly agreed that it would be a good project, but I could tell it seemed monumental to him. I suggested he deal with nine items on the table—move them, throw them out, give them away, or file them. Doing this for nine days could make an incredible impact on his space. Nine items didn't seem too bad. Even the nine days didn't seem too much to ask.

While still in the kitchen, I relayed the story about the Chinese belief that if the burners on the stove were working and clean, he could expect more money and better health. Additionally, cooking good, nutritious food improved a person's health. Therefore it was important for the stovetop burners to be in good working order. From the looks of the stove, I could assume that the possibility of having all four burners in working condition, even if they were scrubbed clean, was slim. Dealing with that stove was going to be a major project.

I could see Ned had had enough suggestions. I figured if I continued he would be overwhelmed. Ned was anxious to schedule another time for me to return. Was that a little enthusiasm behind his quiet demeanor?

As I returned home, I recalled the obstacles I had encountered on my first visit to Ned's place. Returning to my house, I drove by a field of wildflowers and remarked on their beauty — the first sign of spring and new beginnings. What a contrast to my first visit!

As I was driving to Ned's house the next time, I couldn't help thinking how different this appointment was from all of the others I do. Without words, he had made it quite obvious that he needed to incorporate changes slowly, steadily, and in small steps. He also liked the fact that someone was monitoring his progress. I was curious as to what he did with his stove and kitchen table.

Ned greeted me, but didn't look pleased. I feared he might have gone into overload and become discouraged. He explained that his frustration was directed toward the stove which had become a bigger project than we had anticipated. In trying to fix one of the burners, he had disconnected the stove and pulled it out into the middle of the kitchen. He then realized fixing it wasn't something he could do on his own and called a repairman. The stove sat there for over a week while Ned waited for him to show up. With the stove in the middle of the kitchen, it was impossible to move around.

Ned seemed disappointed that he hadn't accomplished everything we had talked about. We discussed the significance of getting to the bottom of a situation that hadn't been right since he had moved in. He knew it would feel good to get that part of his life in order.

As I turned around to see what else he had accomplished, I saw a spotless round table with four matching chairs placed neatly around it. He seemed quite satisfied with himself and found it funny that I was so surprised—shocked might be a better word. The huge table that had been piled full of clutter was cleared and the leaves had been removed. Somewhere he had unearthed a tablecloth (never mind the cigarette burn) and had graciously set out two bottles of spring water and a package of Oreos. I dare say I was probably his first dinner guest.

While enjoying the Oreos, Ned admitted that he had never slept so well as he did now in his new bedroom. He had placed a little plant by the window and enjoyed the effect it had on the space.

It seemed peaceful there that afternoon, despite the stacks of things that were still scattered around. When I commented on this, he told me that his noisy tenants had agreed to move out without any explanation or further trouble. His new tenants were great. They worked all day and were very quiet in the evening. He was delighted by the change, and speculated that maybe the crystal he hung in the center of his house may have created some kind of field that caused the bad tenants to move out and the new good tenants to move in. He started to chuckle at the idea and then stopped, realizing it might actually be true.

Ned and I looked around at the rest of his space. His next concern was the front bedroom where he used to sleep. He had decided to make it into an office. He didn't think he'd use it, but wanted it anyway. He had already begun building bookshelves along one side of the room. He got excited about putting his computer in there with some books and a desk. We talked about the position of the desk. I suggested it be situated so that, when he was sitting there, he would be able to see the door to the room. This meant the desk would be out in the middle of the room, which didn't seem practical to Ned. I also recommended that he curb some of his enthusiasm for building the bookshelves to the ceiling. By lowering the height of the shelves, he wouldn't feel so overwhelmed when he was in the room.

The bookcases would in the end be a significant tool for Ned. It would enable him to sort through his books and old magazines and make some decisions. Despite his excitement about having plenty of bookshelves, I suggested he not build so many. That way, he would be forced to think twice about which books he wanted to keep. Less is more.

Like the bedroom, we discovered that the rag of a carpet concealed a beautiful hardwood floor. Ned had decided on a soft coral color for the walls and together we decided a small strip of track lighting would work for him. I could tell he wanted me to leave so he could get started on this room.

Although I wasn't sure why he wanted me to come back, I agreed on a final visit within a few weeks. He was insistent that I see his beautiful new office when it was done. As I drove back home, I thought that maybe I'd cancel our appointment since this was such a long drive, and instead chat with Ned on the phone to see how he was doing. After a week or so, I decided to keep our appointment. I had to admit I was anxious to see how his office was shaping up. Besides he might have some of those Oreos left.

This fourth and final visit with Ned was really just the beginning for my new friend. All he had needed was a starting point. Once he began to see and feel the difference in energy, he didn't need my input anymore. As I was driving to his house, I reflected how Ned proved to be a great teacher for me—about process, productivity, and patience (mine and his). I knew I couldn't keep driving out to see him every few weeks—sooner or later he would need to assume his own power.

The last time I was there Ned was about to set up the office in his house. I didn't have to wonder how things were going. When I drove up he was coming out the front door with a couple of bags to throw into a dumpster he had parked in front of his duplex. He looked pretty proud of himself as he waved at me. It seems the office project, although not quite complete, had led to a major sorting and de-cluttering bonanza. Three bookshelves were done and in place with selected books placed neatly on them. As Ned found the energy to sort through his books and magazines, he realized he was going to need a dumpster to haul away all the old stuff.

In one of my earlier visits, I had casually suggested a Feng Shui adjustment in dealing with clutter: remove nine items a day for nine days. At the time I wasn't sure that Ned was paying attention to the suggestion since he hadn't responded or written it down. But he had listened. Due to the amount of clutter, each of the nine items for him was a bag filled with useless stuff. Every day he had been taking out nine bags of stuck and stagnant energy, releasing some old and painful ties to the past. Six days (fifty-four bags) had passed since he began this process. Ned was exuberant and almost unrecognizable!

He couldn't walk me into his house fast enough. His plans for the office were becoming elaborate, but not overdone. He showed me the repaired stove, the kitchen table still relatively uncluttered (placemats, too!), new blinds for his bedroom, a new rug for his office. I couldn't believe the change in the place, evidenced in Ned's new energy. He had furniture in his living room I hadn't been able to see before. We discussed some kind of storage system in his closets since clearly there were items he wanted to keep.

We spent about thirty minutes together moving some of his living room furniture to make it more inviting. All of the furniture had been pushed up against the walls, so I suggested pulling the couch away from the window and angling a chair on one side. He would eventually need some additional lighting and a coffee table. But for now, he had a place to sit and relax. I left that day without another appointment set in the future. I felt a little sad, but had been reassured he would invite me back in the near future.

Ned called a few months later to say that after he got the office set up, he was promoted from production to sales at his company. As he would be working from home, he needed that office after all.

We explored the idea of a new relationship for a moment. He decided that he needed to find himself, let go of the past, and create some of his own dreams before getting involved with anyone else's.

It's now been over a year since our visits together. During a recent phone conversation, he told me he is still sleeping well, eats dinner at his kitchen table, and has a cat whose company he enjoys. But the most startling change in Ned's life occurred one morning. He woke up and habitually reached for his cigarettes. Since he was forced to get up in search of matches, he looked around the living room and was struck by the beautiful space he had created. It was orderly, uncluttered, and energetic. He realized that this was not the home of a smoker. That morning he quit cigarettes. If he ever felt any pangs to start again, he just needed to look around at his space. He had created a new message for himself—one that did not include this addiction. As Ned de-cluttered his house, he de-cluttered other baggage in his life, like smoking. Neither of us expected this change, proof that your space reflects your life, the basic Feng Shui principle.

One final note: right before writing Ned's story, I called to see what was going on. He was dating someone and was madly in love. Go, Ned!

Deserving Abundance: What's in the Garage?

Jeanette and Will's Story

Jeanette e-mailed me to set up an appointment. By the time I arrived at her house, we had communicated several more times by e-mail. Her husband Will was present at the appointment. It was obvious he had doubts about the expense involved.

His job had been downsized, even though he'd worked there for twenty years, and he had been given another position. His salary was reduced, but he took the new job until he could figure out another alternative. Jeanette was a real estate agent, but for some reason, in the past six months when they needed the money the most, her sales had hit rock bottom. Because they were not making ends meet, they had been borrowing on their credit cards.

Will and Jeanette had bought their house five years earlier under ideal terms due to Jeanette's connections. They purchased it from a bank as foreclosed property. The first owners relinquished ownership due to their own severe financial difficulties. Will and Jeanette were concerned about any lingering energy from their predecessors.

There was an attached double car garage on the side of the house that reflected the energy of Knowledge, Family, and Wealth *(see First*

Floor Plan). It was so full of belongings that their two cars couldn't fit in the garage. I commented on the condition of this space and the importance of keeping it in order. Will explained that there were about six or seven boxes in the garage that they had never opened. Jeanette took vigorous issue with that comment, assuring me that they *had* been opened. There were simply things in there they didn't need right now. She couldn't remember what they were, but she was sure they might need them some time.

I tried to assure her that the boxes contained items that simply weren't useful to them or they would have used them. The garage was stagnant, dead—just the kind of energy they didn't need in the Wealth part of their space. Storage was fine as long as they knew what they were storing and as long as it was something they wanted in their lives. If they wanted storage space, the boxes should be labeled.

It wasn't just those boxes. I began to ask about their plan for the miscellaneous furniture, bikes, and recycling in the garage. Well, they didn't have a plan. Jeanette's son had his own apartment and she hoped he might want some of the furniture, but so far he hadn't expressed any interest. The garage seemed as good a place as any to store these

GARAGE

KITCHEN

DINING ROOM

PARLOR/ DEN

UP

LIVING ROOM

ENTRY

First Floor Plan

things. Of course, last winter it was more than a little annoying when one car had to sit outside all the time.

I strongly urged that they begin by working on the garage, get rid of the stuff, sweep, and organize it. I went so far as to suggest painting the garage floor to facilitate sweeping it out. Due to their financial state, Will and Jeanette were willing to try anything.

I also noticed that behind the boxes was a door leading from the garage to the back yard. "Never use the door," they chimed. I explained that having a back door in the Wealth area allowed money to get away, whether the door was used or not. Besides, once they'd cleared the stuff out of the way, they might find themselves going in and out of that door. For a back door in Wealth, a recommended adjustment is to hang a wind chime by the door, either inside or outside. A wind chime "calls" the money back into their lives. We walked around the garage to see what was going on in the back yard. A beautiful little maple tree was growing about twelve feet from the garage. One of its branches reached out toward the garage and the door in question. Jeanette decided a wind chime could be hung on that branch to resolve the money issue. She stood and looked around the area as though she were seeing it for the first time. "Why don't we put a little bench out here, maybe the birdbath that we stored somewhere in the garage?" I encouraged any attempts at improving the space.

Another Wealth challenge was a staircase that came from the second floor and landed right in front of the front door. This feature presents another escape route for money—it is propelled out the door at great speed. I suggested that a round, faceted crystal be hung from the light fixture in the entry. The fixture was halfway between the door and the bottom step. A crystal would help slow the Wealth energy from flying out the door. A round rug could also detour the flow of money. Or, because their entry was fairly good-sized, they could place an empty basket by the front door to catch all their money before it had a chance to leave. The basket needed to remain empty at all times and not become the repository for mail, keys, or mittens, I explained. If the basket became filled with items, there would be less room for money. Will and Jeanette opted for hanging the crystal.

It's not uncommon to see the same message transmitted repeatedly throughout a space. Thus far, Will and Jeanette had their Wealth area full of stuck energy in the garage. They had a back door leading money out of their lives, and there was a staircase by the front door. All of these features suggest a potential financial challenge for them.

In addition, their predecessors had had a serious issue with money. We still had the kitchen and their bedroom to address.

There's a Chinese story that suggests a connection between cooking and money: If a person is preparing a fire for cooking food, it is safe to assume that he must have had some money to buy the food. If the person were preparing two, three, or even four fires, he must have had three or four times more money to buy so much food. In modern times, the burners on a stovetop represent the traditional fire and likewise hold the symbol for money. Only two of the four burners on Jeanette and Will's stove worked. They lost half of their money symbolically as well as in reality. The importance of getting the burners fixed was a low priority since they had been eating out almost every meal—until lately when budget constraints necessitated they eat at home more frequently. Will thought it might be something he could fix himself.

When we got to their bedroom *(see Second Floor Plan),* they realized how uncanny this had become. Once Jeanette and Will discovered the messages about money challenges that seemed so prevalent in their space they understood why their lives had taken such a drastic turn financially. In the back left corner of their bedroom, I noticed a large stain on the ceiling. A roof leak, that had been fixed on the outside, but was still evident on the inside. Leaking water is equivalent to leaking money. On top of that, a wastebasket was in that corner, metaphorically throwing away any money they might have. Will decided to start repairing and painting the ceiling. Jeanette pounced on the wastebasket, moving it to another part of the room.

We initially decided the Knowledge area of the room would be fine since Knowledge was currently not an issue for either of them. When she moved the wastebasket, however, she noticed some mold on the

Second Floor Plan

carpet. They surmised that the mold had started when water leaked down from the ceiling. The message around stagnant money once again made itself obvious.

Will and Jeanette were very clear. They wanted to return to the income they had before Will's job was downsized and before Jeanette's business had decreased. I suggested they buy nine Chinese coins since the number nine is a symbol of success and power. I instructed them to tie three of the coins together with a nine-inch red ribbon and place one set in the Wealth area of Jeanette's desk at work. Then I wanted them to tie three more coins together and place another set in the Wealth area of Will's desk. The remaining three coins would be placed singly under their welcome mat by their front door to set a theme of abundance and prosperity in their lives.

Because money issues were evidenced in their jobs, I suggested a plant in their Career area to represent the growth they desired in their respective fields.

"Should we simply move?" they asked. "Wouldn't it be easier?" I discouraged a discussion on their moving, for I was concerned they would merely take their issues with them. Instead, I felt it was important for them to stay where they were in order to address whatever money challenges they were experiencing.

Jeanette and I had an opportunity to talk six months after our appointment. They had fixed the burners on the stove and had repaired the ceiling in their bedroom. They had hung a small, round crystal from the light in their entry. But it wasn't until they began clearing out a few things from the garage that Jeanette noticed an immediate shift in her real estate business. By the time the garage was done, she had surpassed her goals and was back on track. An interesting aside was that in clearing the old furniture out of the garage, she ran across her grandmother's china wrapped up in a box. Jeanette had forgotten it was there. Because she had no use for it, she had it appraised. The china was worth $5000. She eventually sold it to an antique dealer for $4950.

Will, however, struggled for quite some time in his job. Whenever he had an interview arranged, something would come up to prevent him from getting there. One day he was sick; one day the car overheated on the way to the interview, making him an hour-and-a-half late; and one day he just plain forgot. Meanwhile, Jeanette noticed how, after all their work, Will was starting to put things in the garage again. It seemed as if self-sabotage was going on.

Jeanette encouraged him to seek counseling around this issue. Will discovered that, having grown up in a poor family, and watching his parents sacrifice and struggle, he believed he didn't deserve an easier life. Rather than seeing an increased flow of money as an opportunity to help out his parents who were both living, he saw it as an insult to his upbringing. It was a hard, but real revelation which Will continues to work on today. To assist him in this process, he works conscientiously to keep their garage in order. If his outer wealth message reflects order and flow, he can more easily take in the new order and flow on the inner level as well. He can always tell if he's falling back into his old limited ways of thinking and feeling by the state of the garage.

Building a Dream

Ray and Angela's Story

I was called by a couple, Ray and Angela, who were looking to build a home. They had blueprints from their architect and wanted me to look at them. Unfortunately, they were on their final draft and were not open to making many changes. Their architect had been invited to our meeting but declined. His perspective was that Feng Shui would only complicate their process, which had been going smoothly. Additionally, there was no scientific proof, according to him, that adding any Feng Shui adjustments would make any positive difference. Nevertheless, Ray and Angela wanted another perspective, but they quietly hoped I wouldn't suggest they change anything.

Ray and Angela were empty nesters. All of their children were grown and married. However, they had decided to move from a smaller home to this bigger one. Ray and Angela wanted their children and grandchildren to visit frequently during holidays and other times of the year. They had specifically built an apartment above their garage for these occasions.

Ray had taken early retirement so they could travel. Despite good investments and a generous retirement package, they were concerned about having enough money to last them the rest of their years. Although they were both in fairly good health, Ray had been experiencing digestive problems.

When I looked at their layout according to the bagua *(see Proposed Plan)*, it was clear to me that Ray and Angela were building a home with their children in mind. The Children and Creativity area was extended out beyond normal boundaries, indicating extra energy around this issue. The garage was also an extension, although it was still an over-sized piece added onto the house, coming off the Knowledge area. I asked about their youngest son. Angela looked surprised that I asked about him since he would probably be using the guest area the most. He had three children of his own, lived the farthest away, and was the one most likely to visit on a regular basis. Ray and Angela had made their decision about the guest area to accommodate his needs, and even referred to it as "Patrick's Place." The room was appropriately situated in the knowledge area, reflecting the energy of the youngest son.

I did express concern that the garage, "Patrick's Place," was coming off the house at an angle which could set up frenzy. This may not reflect in Patrick's life because he would only be a visitor, but would most likely reflect in Ray and Angela's lives. The lot size did not permit

DECK

EATING
AREA

MASTER
BDRM.

LIVING
ROOM

KITCHEN

UP

DINING
RM.

LAUN.

STUDY

GARAGE

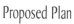

ENTRY

Proposed Plan

them to "straighten out" the garage, so I suggested they mark the spot where the garage would be if it had been built straight across. They had to imagine it could be swung around to be flush with the front of their house. On that spot (✱) they could plant a tree or a flag, possibly a bird bath. They were open to any number of suggestions.

However, when superimposing the bagua on this revised layout, not only would they be missing all of Wealth, there would be considerable pieces missing in Fame, Health, and Family. They had clearly expressed concern about maintaining their wealth. In addition to marking where the garage would be, Ray and Angela would need to mark the furthermost corner to square off the space (♦).

The angle dilemma was also apparent in their eating area. The breakfast room had been built with angled walls to capture a view of the lake. Yet the feature sets up fast activity, not usually in a way that is welcome. I pointed out that they had built a lovely hint of an octagon in their master bedroom and suggested they change the breakfast area to mirror that shape. It would give a symmetry to their home, plus it wouldn't obstruct any views to the lake.

Their concern for health prompted some suggestions regarding their foyer. Having the dining room so close to the front entrance sets up digestive problems, not to mention reflecting a pattern of inadequate support when support is needed. People have a tendency to come to eat, but have a quick way out when so close to the front door. Additionally, there is a powder room on the other side of the foyer which is another digestive problem. The drain from the toilet takes away the occupants' health. In order to diminish both of those challenges, I suggested that the entrance to the dining room from the foyer either be walled in or have doors which could be closed. And I suggested that the door to the powder room would have to be kept closed as well.

The architect had positioned a bathroom toilet exactly behind the stove. It doesn't take a lot of imagination to realize that those two energies do not mix well. I suggested they move their stovetop to the island. Since they've used that partial octagon shape so often in the kitchen already, I strongly encouraged them to make the island an octagon also. Not only would the stovetop be away from the toilet, it would also enable the cook to get a better view of the entrance to the kitchen. Whether coming from the garage or the front door, people would not catch the cook off guard. Cooking with your back to entrances leaves the cook susceptible to surprises. This metaphor not only applies to cooking, but, in a bigger picture, to life in general.

In their bedroom, which was very auspiciously placed in the Partnership area of their space, we discussed the positioning of their bed. It seemed obvious to place it on the outside wall so they could have a view of their entrances as well as out the windows in the octagonal bay area.

Having the library by the front door is a good position for this room. It is a strong statement about the intellectual interests of Ray and Angela and leaves a good first impression.

Ray and Angela went back to their architect with the suggestions I had made. When I saw the final drawings *(see Final Plan),* they had incorporated all the proposed changes along with some additional ones of their own. The biggest change was that the garage was no longer situated at an angle. When I asked about this change, both Ray and Angela were quick to tell me the architect hadn't liked that feature all along. He didn't know exactly why, but was very happy to have an excuse to make a change (♦). They still needed to adjust for a missing piece in the Wealth area.

They closed off the opening to the dining room, creating a lighted alcove in the wall in which to display artwork. Upon reflection, Ray and Angela realized that they didn't need a formal dining room. They were quite certain it would never get used. So what had been the dining room became the laundry room and the powder room. They bought a table for the breakfast area that could be expanded to accommodate visitors as needed. This being their Wealth area, they decided that the more frequent use of this eating area would be beneficial.

Final Plan

The master bathroom had been re-configured to allow the powder room by the front door to sit further away from the foyer. A privacy wall had also been installed to ensure no influence from the toilet would be possible. During the building process, I suggested that they drop nine Chinese coins in each of the corners of their house so that "wealth" would be built right into the walls of their new home.

The house held a more balanced and more stable feel. Ray and Angela have been enjoying their space for several years now. As they had hoped, their children frequently return, filling their home with excitement and activity. "Patrick's Place" has been used not only by Ray and Angela's other children, but also by one of Ray's brothers who needed a place to live while his life was in transition. Their health continues strong and steady as do their financial investments.

An Office on the Move

Marty's Story

Marty got my name from an article in a local newspaper. He was division president of a major corporation that was about to move into new headquarters. A frequent visitor to Hong Kong, Marty knew the importance of Feng Shui in his business dealings there, so he decided to have someone check out his new building. He paid for the consultation personally; he didn't want his staff to know about it.

We set up a time to meet at the new building. It was still under construction, but the walls would be going up soon. He thought this would be a good time to think about the offices and which staff members would occupy which offices. He made it clear to me on the phone that he wanted to meet me privately and he expressed more than once the importance of confidentiality.

You can imagine my surprise when I showed up at the site and saw Marty with five people. His secretary Lisa had gotten wind of the appointment and asked to come along. And as the word spread, a man from engineering asked to come along as well, then one of the vice presidents and finally two people from building maintenance. They all assured me that they had come along just to listen. Within ten minutes I could tell this was not a listening bunch of people. They each one had their own agenda and wanted me to look at their own potential offices or cubicles, hoping I'd give them the advice they'd need to change their lives.

I kept checking in with Marty to see if he wanted me to be handling this some other way. After all, he was paying for this appointment personally. He had evidently resigned himself to the direction the consultation was going. He graciously allowed each person some time alone with me. In fact, he even wandered off, looking at the progress in other areas of the building. When his secretary Lisa and I began discussing the placement of her office, however, it was imperative that Marty become involved because her choice of office was going to affect his.

Marty had intended to move into an office near the front entrance. He was very much a people person and wanted to be involved in the comings and goings near the front desk. He figured it would be handy for the people who came to see him—they wouldn't have to walk very far to his office. Lisa would also be stationed near the front since she was his executive secretary.

I explained to Marty that, as the boss, as the visionary, he needed to take an anchor spot in the space. He needed to be in a strong driving position to lead this huge division to success and profitability. The command position was not in the front of the office, but in the back corner furthest from the front entrance. The back office I was suggesting according to the layout was a corner one, giving Marty vision in many directions, both in reality and in metaphor. It was one of the biggest offices and seemed appropriate for his title and his job. Marty was planning on making it a conference room for that very reason—it was the biggest room.

All five people were rapt with attention as we discussed Marty's position in the company. He still opted to be near the front, however. From a Feng Shui perspective, people situated near the front entrance of a business, unless they're sales people, tend not to stay around. The energy of the coming and going that naturally occurs in a reception area can sweep anyone nearby away. This is why receptionist positions can have a high rate of turnover. Remembering how Marty wanted this appointment to be private, I couldn't say this in front of his employees.

Without saying these exact words, I tried to impress on Marty the importance of being in the back of the office. At times, I must have seemed adamant. I finally decided I'd just call him and have a private conversation about the matter. I suggested a phone follow-up in a couple days and, although open to it, he informed me that he would be leaving in two days and would be gone almost until their move-in date. I stressed that I would contact him before he left. He was fine with that.

I called three different times. Each time Lisa graciously took the message, assured me she was giving him his messages, but also assured me that Marty was extremely busy. In her friendly way, appropriate to her position, she insisted that if I just shared with her the reason for my call, she might be able to act as a liaison. Of course, I wasn't going to share my concerns: "Look, Lisa, your boss is sitting too close to the door. It's possible that he's either going to quit or get fired." Marty left on his travels and we never had a chance to speak to one another.

Four months after our appointment, a casual glance through the morning newspaper presented some astounding news, although not surprising. The lead story in the business section was about Marty's company. An internal upheaval had come to a head, and Marty resigned. He had occupied his new office exactly one month before leaving abruptly.

A week after the news article, Marty left a message for me on my voicemail. He let me know he was starting his own company and wanted some advice. I met him again, this time under totally different circumstances. For one thing, we were alone, and this time his office was small and efficient. He was beginning a new company with one other person.

He admitted that during our original appointment he knew I had sensed he might quit his job. He had been planning to resign for over a year, but once he got into the new building, it happened more quickly than he had expected. Marty told me that if the five people had not been present, he and I might have had a totally different experience. Although he regretted the outcome of our appointment, he knew that his life had unfolded appropriately.

His new office was smaller in size and held fewer people. Marty was the majority partner, so we selected the office that was in the command position. We made sure he had room to position a desk so that he would be facing the entry door to the office. The only issue apparent in his new digs was that his office was located on the fifteenth floor of a large office building with floor to ceiling windows, providing no support for the people trying to work there. I suggested placing his desk in such a way that Marty would have his back to these windows. We needed to make sure he could pull his desk forward so he could have either a credenza behind him as he sat at his desk or at least some tall plants to provide a wall of security. A credenza seemed to be the most practical.

By placing him in the command position, Marty wound up right next door to the public bathrooms. Although he wasn't sharing a wall with any of the toilets or urinals, he was afraid he'd be bothered by the sound of all the flushing. I suggested a fountain be brought into his office to provide some soothing background sound. The bubbling of a fountain could mask the bathroom noises sufficiently so he wouldn't be distracted. Besides, a fountain would symbolize the flow of money in his new business venture.

Marty confirmed that they were not going to hire a receptionist until it was warranted. I wondered how he would know whether anyone had walked in the front door since his new office and his partner's were situated so that neither man could see someone coming in. Marty figured the two of them would listen for the door opening and whoever wasn't tied up on the phone or involved with another client would get up and greet the visitor. The problem with that theory, I assured both men, was that the space was carpeted and the door opened silently. They would both have to check the reception area on a regular basis in case anyone had walked in. They would have to get up and walk out into the hallway. Marty didn't like the idea of a bell on the door as it reminded him of a little retail shop. He thought he might like a buzzer of some sort. I encouraged him to make sure the buzzer was not startling. He would not want to walk out to meet someone if he looked annoyed.

Marty discussed the color of the carpet with me, since the existing carpet was going to be replaced by the management of the building. Based on the Chinese Five Elements theory, Marty's height and pioneering spirit assured me that his wood element was in high gear. To support his new business, I suggested a gray or green color (gray is a water color, which would support his wood; green is a wood color, which would add to his natural element). I also suggested he purchase, as an abundance adjustment, three, six, or nine Chinese coins and place them on the floor before the new carpet was laid. The coins would be most effective being placed near the entrance to their space. This theme of financial success would be energetically present the moment someone walked in.

Marty proudly showed me their new logo—modern, sleek, and encased in a circle. It was very indicative of the cutting edge business he was creating. I suggested that they might want to cut the design into the carpet in the center of their space. The center was in a hallway, not far from the front entrance. He bought the idea with enthusiasm. He figured if they moved on to another place, they could patch the hole in the carpet so the future tenants would never know it had existed. I assured him that placing a round shape near the center would help to bring balance and harmony to his new business. After all the turmoil of his past job, balance and harmony sounded refreshing to Marty.

I also suggested that, if possible, Marty and his partner incorporate the five colors associated with the Five Elements in the reception area—red, yellow, black, white, and green. When all five colors are used within a space, there is an automatic sense of balance and unity. We figured that if Marty chose gray carpet (black), moved in a couple of large plants (green), used wood furnishings (tan/yellow), then accented it with red and white, he would achieve that balance. Red flowers in a reception area are desirable to keep the energy moving. He liked that idea. He also decided that he could keep the walls a white or off-white to bring the final element color into play.

We selected an auspicious date to open the business—one based on Chinese astrology. I left him that day, having had quite a different experience from our first appointment. His new business far surpassed his expectations. Within a year Marty had to move to bigger offices and expanded his staff to six. Along the way, he's been careful to keep himself in the driver's seat by locating his office in a back corner. An outdoorsman at heart, he mentioned to me that being in the back of his space makes sense to him, for, like paddling a canoe, the steering must come from the back.

Finding the New in the Old

Marilyn and Don's Story

Marilyn and Don called me on the recommendation of some friends. They were about to finalize a deal on their current house and within the month would be closing on another house they wanted to buy. They thought some Feng Shui advice at this stage would be a good idea.

I met them at the new place to look around. Although it was empty, the house still exuded a lot of charm and beauty, and I could see why they were drawn to it. Nevertheless, I was at a distinct disadvantage. I couldn't see what they owned and where they were planning to position their belongings. However, they were able to describe to me in great detail the various pieces of furniture they had and where they envisioned placing them.

I asked about the predecessor in the home and whether they knew why it was being sold. Marilyn and Don were buying it from a young widow whose husband had died of a heart attack while watching television at home one evening. That's why she was selling the house. As they were relaying this story, I noticed a missing corner in the Partnership area of this house. I pointed this out to them and discussed what they might do to minimize the impact of this feature. I also spoke to them about the impact of having someone die in the house. The widow had told them a family minister had been out to bless the house before she put it on the market. Both Marilyn and Don felt as though this was sufficient to clear the house.

Of the two of them, Don was far more excited about this new place. At least he was outwardly expressing his enthusiasm more than Marilyn was. He was quick to show me all the features he liked about the house. He could see his workbench in one area of the basement and his recliner by the window. He loved the attached garage. Their current home didn't have a garage. Actually, there wasn't much Don didn't like about this house.

Marilyn was more subdued. "What's your favorite feature?" I finally asked her. She shrugged, surprised at my question. "I like it all," she said noncommittally. "Is there one room you like most of all?" I pressed her. "They're all fine," she assured me. "Are you thinking of painting any of the rooms?" Marilyn clearly hadn't thought about it. While she pondered the question, Don jumped in with the answers. Painting was definitely in the plan. In fact, it was so elaborate and dramatic, I found it interesting that Marilyn didn't know about it. When he was done describing the painting plans,

I turned to Marilyn and asked, "Are you okay with that?" "Sure," she said flatly.

Something was going on here. Synchronistically, Don got a call on his cell phone. The connection wasn't very good so he had to shout into the phone. He stepped outside so we wouldn't be disturbed. I looked at Marilyn. "Are you happy about this move?" I kept my voice low. Marilyn looked me straight in the eye and said, "Look, if Don's happy, I'm happy." That wasn't what I'd asked her. "Do you even like this place?" "It's okay," she said. "Do you like your old house better?" I guessed. Marilyn's eyes filled with tears. "I love the house we're in. It breaks my heart to think of leaving it. But Don wants to move. He's sure that if I get in here, I'll learn to love this place, too."

Don came back inside. Marilyn reached for a tissue. I stared at their missing piece in Partnership. We talked about a few more ideas for floor coverings before my time was up. Marilyn and Don estimated that they would be closing on their old house within the week, two weeks at the most. The closing for the new place hadn't been set yet, but they were hopeful it could occur a day sooner.

Before we left that day, we arranged another appointment, giving them a few weeks to settle in. As a parting thought, I suggested that they hang a ceramic wind chime in the Partnership area of their current home. I figured that they could begin activating the energy of their Partnership in their old home, in anticipation of moving into a place where it would be challenged. In my own mind, I speculated that in energizing the relationship between them, Marilyn might find her own voice and speak up about her wishes. Sometimes activating the energy in an area can bring a situation to the surface and force a shift. They both assured me that they could hang a wind chime for the remaining days in their space.

One week after our initial visit, Don called me. The anxiety in his voice was evident. It seems that Marilyn had let him know that she didn't want to move. The night after they hung their wind chime she erupted during supper. Don was taken off guard, for he hadn't noticed her sadness whenever they talked about the new place.

But that wasn't all. While the two of them were discussing the situation over dinner, the real estate agent called to say the people who wanted to buy their home didn't qualify. The closing was off. Because their current home wasn't selling, they could not move forward on the new house. They were in no position financially to maintain ownership on two houses. Everything was off. They wouldn't be moving any time soon. The events had been arranged so carefully, he said. He couldn't figure out what happened. Coincidentally things seemed to fall apart once the wind chime got in place. Did I have any ideas?

I suggested leaving the wind chime in place. I assured Don that there was always a bigger plan in life and to trust that everything was going as it should. He countered by saying that the only good he could see in this turn of events was that he wasn't going to have to clean off his desk in order to move.

He couldn't hide his disappointment, although he certainly didn't want to leave a house that Marilyn felt so strongly about. Evidently, over the years of their marriage, some patterns of dysfunctional communication had settled in, he admitted. He had been certain he knew his wife well and knew what was best for both of them. But during one eventful dinner he found that he didn't know her well at all. He felt bad about it. He wanted me to come to their current home. They had to regroup.

I suggested that he proceed with his plans to clean off his desk. Horizontal surfaces hold the potential for vision and creativity. The more a surface is cluttered and filled, the less vision is available.

Clearing the top of his work space could bring him some clarity and insight that he wanted, not to mention creativity. He agreed to do so.

When I arrived at Marilyn and Don's house later, they were sitting on their porch. The two of them walked me around the space, but this time Marilyn actively participated in the conversation. She clearly was invested in the house. Don, too, shared some fond memories of the space. Their wind chime was still in place. Don still maintained that the wind chime was somehow responsible for their change in direction. He tried to put a positive spin on the situation by admitting that maybe moving into a place where a man had just died and where there were potential Partnership problems was not such a good thing.

I asked him his biggest disappointment in losing the new house. He was sad about the workbench area, and he really hated not having an attached garage. In the house they were living in, that wasn't possible. Ultimately Don had perceived the move to a different home as a new beginning for Marilyn and him.

When we entered the office, Don was quick to excuse the look of his desk. He hadn't cleaned it off yet. Without the urgency of a move, he had lost heart and didn't tackle it. He didn't see the point. I wanted to re-frame the activity of cleaning off the desk so that it became more than just a task. I suggested he consider cleaning his desk as a way to decide the answer to whether to look for another home or stay in their present one. Doing so, he might find a creative solution. "Like some plans for an addition to this house?" he asked jokingly. "You might be surprised," I teased him.

Their house was basically rectangular with a detached garage out in back. I could see why they might want to start over because most of the decorating (wallpaper, carpet, paint) needed updating. Marilyn admitted it had been over twenty years since they had fixed up any of the rooms. I made many suggestions, trying to prioritize what would have the most impact. I didn't want them to get discouraged, but something needed to shift. At the top of the list was Don's desk. Somehow that felt important—probably because he was resisting it. This time Don promised he would certainly clean the desk looking for the answer to their problem.

I also got them focused on their bedroom, believing that if they could update the room, it would affect all aspects of their lives. We spent some time brainstorming about favorite colors, themes, and new furniture. Marilyn looked as though new life had been breathed into her.

Two weeks later Don called. "You won't believe this. I cleaned off my desk and in one of the stacks was a house plan I had torn out of a magazine years ago. I kept it because it gave me an idea for an addition to the back of a house that looked a lot like ours. We've already spoken to a contractor about the possibility of adding onto our house. With the equity we've acquired over the years, we're going to proceed. You were right. The answer was on my desk all along."

Don elaborated on the details, describing how, by tearing down the old garage, they could rebuild a new one off the kitchen. The garage would be large enough for a workshop. His enthusiasm came through loud and clear. Marilyn was relieved and delighted. They wanted to set up an appointment so I could look at their plans to see if there were any potential problems or concerns.

But that wasn't all. Don had another matter to discuss. He asked if I had heard the news about the other house. It had burned down a week or so ago. I told him I had heard something about it but hadn't paid much attention to the story. The fire took place in the middle of the night. It was considered a total loss. Don's voice tensed. That was the house he wanted to buy! Luckily, the new owners weren't home at the time of the fire, but Marilyn and Don might not have been as fortunate. The big plan had definitely been at work for them.

Before hanging up, Don said, "How does this stuff work, this Feng Shui stuff? It seems like you do something unrelated to what you're trying to work on and it unfolds something else. You hang a wind chime and it saves your life. You clean your desk and you add a garage." "Yeah, that's about how it works," I responded. "Just keep your wind chime in place and keep your desk clear and you'll be okay, Don." There was no argument with him on that account.

Moving On after a Loss

Ever since she moved into her home four years ago, Anne explained, tragedy had been her constant companion. Within six months, her husband Frank had been killed in a car accident, her son Nelson came close to flunking out of high school, and she had been downsized at work. Although she had a job, the pay wasn't adequate, and she might be forced to look for another job. Money was a serious concern, as her husband's life insurance wasn't very substantial. In addition, Anne had noticed her health was worse. She loved the house, but was seriously considering whether she should move. She asked me directly if I thought the house was possessed.

Anne and Frank had bought the house as a model. Yet even if they had built it themselves, there wasn't much they would have changed. Previously they lived in a smaller home in another part of the city. They had moved because they wanted more space as Frank was beginning to do a lot of work at home and needed an office there. They also wanted to move before Nelson got into high school. The timing seemed right on all counts.

Before even superimposing the bagua on the space, I noticed a few features which could be a problem. First, upon entering, the front entrance lined up directly with two huge glass windows in the back. This feature is a potential for lost opportunities, implying that energy can get into the space, but has a direct route out before it has a chance to bless the owners and the home. The lost energy can affect health, money, relationship, career, etc. Anne needed to find a way to slow down this ch'i highway—a plant in front of the window, a screen by the entrance to block the view, a crystal in the window—something that could do the same thing. Anne moved a hand-carved, wooden, seven-foot piece of sculpture in front of the window. It allowed enough light to get in, but definitely kept one's eye in the space before moving on, out to the porch.

I asked about her use of the formal dining room. "Never" came quickly with certainty. Having a food room (kitchen or dining room) so close to the front door is a potential for health issues. Since she never used the room, it would be better to use it for something else—a library, perhaps, or a music room. Anne was delighted to hear this suggestion, since her parents were planning to give her a grand piano which had been in their family for years. She had been concerned about where she would put such a huge piece of furniture, but hadn't thought of the dining room. She would now have a place to position it beautifully, plus she could eliminate the negative health messages she was getting every day.

Her son Nelson had been sleeping in the front bedroom, which was located in front of the front door. When someone has a bedroom in this configuration, the person occupying that room does not feel as if they're part of the family. There's always a sense of being abandoned. No doubt these feelings were magnified when his father died so abruptly. There was no particular reason Nelson slept in that room, so I suggested he take the middle bedroom, which reflects the strongest energy for the oldest son in a family. Anne could make the front bedroom into a guest room or home office.

In the master bedroom, Anne and Frank had placed their bed with their heads up against the wall holding the fireplace in the great room. This situation is another health-depleting factor: the fireplace burns up the couple's energy. Putting the bed against the opposite wall, common to the walk-in closet, gave Anne a better perspective on life— she could easily see the entrance to her bedroom from both the house and the porch. And, most importantly, it got her away from the fire.

When I laid out the bagua on her house, a few more issues came to light. In the Wealth area, Anne has a lot of drains, possibilities for Wealth to escape—the two sinks, the whirlpool, the toilet, and the shower. I suggested that she get some purple or lavender in the bathroom to counteract the drainage. The walls were already pretty neutral in color, so accenting with a deep eggplant color seemed intriguing to Anne. I also recommended that she plug up the drains when not in use to keep money from getting away.

The fireplace in the breakfast room was not a problem. Adding fire to the Partnership area feeds its energy and supports a loving relationship. Anne confirmed that their marriage had actually improved once they had moved into this house.

We walked out to the porch in the back of the house. Although it has three sides and a roof, it doesn't qualify as part of the bagua. I asked her about screening in the open side, which was something she and Frank were going to do the first summer they were in the house. But she put that on hold when he died. The Fame and Reputation area, which is located over the porch, is considered challenged because so much of it is missing. The Fame and Reputation area is often connected to the Career area at the front of the house. Being

PORCH

BKFST AREA

MASTER BEDROOM

GREAT ROOM

PANTRY

LAUND.

KITCHEN

BEDROOM

DINING ROOM

BEDROOM

GARAGE

ENTRY

downsized or demoted in one's career has connections to a person's reputation. She decided to review the plan of closing in the porch. She had no doubt she would use it more after she screened it in, but she was intrigued about making it even more useful by closing it in. I supported that idea wholeheartedly.

Speaking of Career, that area, too, was challenged due to the set-back of the front door. I encouraged her to paint the door her favorite color. Anne really liked the idea of painting it yellow. Besides communicating to the world her favorite color, it would bring the door "forward" to fill up the missing area of Career. I also suggested that she landscape across the front to fill in the space.

In the kitchen, Anne's sink and stove were directly opposite each other. This situation usually sets up some potential for arguing or disagreements. Living with a teenager, she nodded with a knowledge I could only imagine. I suggested that a round, faceted crystal be hung between the two appliances. Because a vaulted ceiling made this impossible, we explored other options for easing the tension here. I suggested a round rug between the sink and stove. A rug with all five colors of the Five Elements (white, black, green, red, and yellow) would also bring some balance.

The square column or pillar in the dining room was very close to the exact center of the Health area. It made good sense to find a way to enhance that square column. Being the creative person that she is, Anne decided to paint vines going around the column and onto the soffit that denoted the dining room space. She had done some painting herself in the breakfast room, so this idea would work. She agreed to add touches of yellow to the vines to stress the color for Health.

She had both an extension and a missing area in the Helpful People part of her house. The extension that sticks out in front of the bagua line is an extra blessing. The little corner set in on the side is a challenge. Anne has a missing area in the Knowledge corner as well. To square off the Knowledge corner, Anne was most open to placing a shrub in the exact corner of the yard. She agreed to place a small mirror in the garage to "push" the wall forward and complete the missing Helpful People piece.

Because money was her most pressing need, I prioritized what needed to be done. The bathroom should be her first item. She agreed to plug up the drains on the sinks and the bathtub each night. Keeping the lid down on the toilet wasn't a problem. She also offered to get a round plastic drain stop for the shower. She was intrigued by the idea of bringing in some shade of purple or lavender in the bathroom. She was seeing purple candles, lavender towels and a rug. I could see she was getting the idea.

Anne invited me back three months later. She told me that she had been hired by a firm at nearly twice the salary she had been making doing exactly what she loves to do. The best part was that she was able to work at home three days a week. She had transformed the front bedroom into her office.

When I arrived, I couldn't help but notice the lovely yellow front door. Anne had pretty well completed all the things we had discussed. But what she was really thrilled about was how she had transformed her bathroom. She couldn't wait to show me the purple/lavender theme. She was positive that all this intention in the bathroom was what brought about her job. The day she came home with her new rug and placed it on the floor there, the phone rang, and she was offered the job of her dreams. This extra money now made it possible for her to think about closing in the back porch.

Anne had also painted graceful, winding vines on the center pillar of her Health area. Along with the painting, she had added silk vines to give a three-dimensional effect. She had extended the painted vines into the music room where her grand piano was now sitting. Her house was inviting and warm now. As so often happens with clients, I could see a new energy in Anne as well.

Her son Nelson liked his new bedroom very much. Things had eased between Nelson and Anne recently. He was spending a little more time with her and lending a hand when she needed him. Maybe he was beginning to feel like part of the family again.

As we were concluding our time together, Anne asked the question I had been expecting. I could tell she was somewhat reluctant to bring it up. "Do you see any reason why Frank had to die? Could we have seen this coming and taken precautions? Could it have been the front door/back window line-up?" she asked. I assured her the line-up alone would not have led to something so tragic. "Could it have been our headboard against the fireplace wall?" Again, it was hardly a situation that would have caused me alarm. I assured her there was no one thing that contributed to his untimely death. It could have just been the drunk driver who hit Frank's car head-on. Sometimes life holds mysteries we will never resolve. Feng Shui can change or shift some aspects of one's destiny, but there is always a bigger plan which unfolds, no matter what.

The important thing was that she was finding her own life again and moving forward. One year after my second visit to Anne, she called to say that she was getting married and was buying another house with her fiancé, Riley. Anne's excitement was evident over the phone. Nelson would be graduating and going to college, so she wanted to begin anew in another house. She admitted to me that marrying again had never been a goal after Frank's death. But now that it was happening, she knew it was what Frank would want her to do.

Anne and Riley's story appears next.

Beginning Again

Anne and Riley's Story

Anne contacted me because she and her new husband were buying a home. Having remarried after the death of her first husband, Anne wanted to start afresh in a new home, new to both her and Riley. She called me to look at a house they were considering.

I first met with them over a cup of coffee. They brought their blueprints for me to look at since they hadn't been able to contact the people who owned the house to get the keys. They were no longer living there because they had been transferred to Europe. The wife was torn about leaving since she adored the house. She had invested a lot of energy in it, but Europe was attractive. The husband was thrilled to be making this move, as it not only meant new adventures for them, but a substantial promotion.

Anne already had some ideas. A feature she had come to love in her old house was an enclosed back porch *(see Main Floor Plan)*. So, she wanted to enclose the deck, but wasn't sure of the impact on the house. She also wanted to arrange an office for herself, as she worked at home several days a week. They wanted a guest room and a library.

DECK

KITCHEN

DINING AREA

FAMILY ROOM

UP

LIVING ROOM

STUDY

LAUNDRY

GARAGE

Main Floor Plan

They had enough bedrooms to do all this, but they weren't sure what to put where.

There were only a couple of similarities between Anne's old house and this one—the garage projecting out the right side of the house and a setback front door.

The new house was a two-story with all the bedrooms upstairs. The kitchen would be in the Wealth area. I saw that in the center of this home on the first floor there was a powder room as well as a staircase. The toilet was almost exactly in the center of the space. Both the stairs and the bathrooms were a challenge to the health of the family living there. We needed to address this issue first. I assumed neither feature would be moved considering the amount of effort it would take. They assured me that moving the bathroom as well as the stairs had not been in their plans.

A bathroom in the middle of a house can drain away the energy around health, "flushed" of all energy or vitality. There are many possible actions to offset this drain. First, I asked Anne and Riley to try to keep the bathroom door closed at all times. Her objection was that there was no window in there, and it might feel stuffy if the door was kept closed all the time. They were willing to consider it, however.

MASTER BEDRM.

BEDRM. C

BEDRM. B

BEDRM. A

Second Floor Plan

Due to the seriousness of the position of the bathroom in this area, I suggested they hang a mirror on the outside of the bathroom door to bounce back any energy from getting in there and being flushed away. They'd think about that as well.

Anne remembered the bathroom as green, a color she wasn't particularly fond of. Since the color for the center Health area is yellow, I offered the suggestion that she paint the bathroom yellow, or use yellow as an accent color. She agreed to the idea. I also suggested that she get her paint brush out and recreate some of the beautiful vines she painted on the walls in her bathroom and her music room of her former house. I wanted these vines to be growing upwards to counteract the downward flushing action of the toilet and the sink drain. She didn't need any coaxing.

The staircase was also in the center of the Health area. This "up and down" situation could potentially become their health story. When an unevenness is occurring in a space, a round or oval object helps to balance the energy. I suggested that a round rug be placed at the foot of the staircase. Due to the hardwood floors in this house, a rug would be a beautiful addition. They wondered about a round rug at the top of the stairs as well. It wouldn't hurt, I assured them. In fact, a round rug at the top of the stairs would be the Health area of the second floor, so it would be particularly helpful.

As far as room assignments on the second floor, I suggested that Anne's office be in the front bedroom *(Bedroom A)*. This room is partially over the garage, but since it was not being used as a bedroom, I didn't see that as a problem. Sleeping over a garage does not provide enough support for a person and can bring up issues of abandonment and feelings of separation. These feelings can all lead to ill health. But using a room over a garage where a person is awake and conscious does not impact them in this way.

I suggested that the next bedroom *(Bedroom B)* be a guest room and the remaining one *(Bedroom C)* be their library. Guest rooms are appropriately placed near the front end of the house so guests do not feel so welcome they decide they don't want to leave. Both the energy of Anne's work and the energy of guests coming to visit should be separate from Anne and Riley's personal space.

This was all we discussed about their new home on the initial visit. They were planning to finalize the purchase within the month. Meanwhile, Anne was having trouble selling her current home and asked for some suggestions. She hadn't begun packing yet, as she didn't want boxes sitting around when people came to look at the place. I encouraged her to let go of that perception and to begin packing anyway. People would see that she's on her way out and would understand that she's serious about moving.

I also recommended that she begin in the basement where so many old memories are often stored. And I suggested that any pictures of her and her family be carefully packed and put away. She needed to remove anything that had her name on it. In other words, Anne needed to make the space neutral so other people could see themselves in it and not feel they were kicking someone out of their home.

This, of course, would bring up the painful business of sorting through some of Frank's things (her first husband who was killed in a car crash). But, it would have to be done at some point. As soon as she was free of her ties to the past, she would be free to sell the house. I wasn't suggesting she throw out the past, just that she deal with it and sort through it. I could tell Anne understood what I was talking about. Procrastinating wouldn't make it go away.

Since Anne and Riley were beginning a new relationship, I strongly urged that they buy a new bedroom set if financially possible. They had planned to use Riley's, which he had bought a few years ago while he was still married to someone else. I suggested that if they didn't buy an entirely new bedroom set, then at least buy a new mattress and box spring. If not that, then at least new sheets, pillows, and pillowcases. I could tell that Anne definitely did not want his old bedroom set in her new house.

The next time I met them, they had lived in their home for almost six months. They had gotten married, sold both of their homes, and moved into this new one. They both looked radiant as they showed me around their house. One of the first things they did after moving in was to hire a contractor to build a screened porch over the deck. They also extended the deck to go behind the family room. I had assured them that by building the porch, they could extend their Wealth area dramatically. As a deck, without roof and sides, it didn't impact the space in their house. But by enclosing it, the porch influenced the energy in the house, giving them the potential of earning or inviting in more money.

Anne was particularly pleased with the powder room. She had painted the walls a soft yellow and had put her artistic talents to work, painting delicate vines around the mirror over the sink and coming up from around the toilet. She had skillfully painted a few on the opposite wall to balance the effect. The vines had some brighter yellow flowers incorporated along with lavender ones. She had outdone herself and I could feel her pride. They also found a way to keep the door closed by simply putting scented candles in the room. Even unlit they provided a freshness to the room whenever anyone walked in. Riley had put a knocker on the door so someone could knock before walking in. Otherwise, they felt it would be difficult to know if someone was using the bathroom or not since the door was kept closed all the time. They also had the word "Toilette" engraved in script lettering on the knocker in the place where someone's name would ordinarily be located.

A round rug had found a spot at the bottom of the staircase. Anne's office was nicely set up with the desk positioned in such a way she could see the entrance to the room. She could also see if anyone was coming up to her front door on the main level. They did not buy a new bedroom set. Instead, Anne and Riley painted the one he had and all the other furniture an off-white color which gave their bedroom a spacious feeling. They did get a new mattress and boxspring along with new sheets and pillows. Somehow Riley managed to add a poster to each corner of the bed so they could create a canopy over the top. Both of them reassured me that it felt like a whole new set.

As for Anne's job in selling her old house, it was a victory. She admitted that she went through some difficult moments sorting through memories of her past life with Frank. But, for the sake of her new relationship, she knew she had to do so. The real estate agent continued to bring people through the house. Finally, one woman returned again and again. She was always alone and seemed very tentative. So Anne was surprised when the woman made an offer for the house. When she questioned the agent, she was told that this woman was a recent widow, raising a son by herself. Anne couldn't help but see the parallel to her own life. She and the woman agreed on a selling price quickly and honorably. The woman wanted to come by on several occasions to check out certain things. Anne was happy to accommodate her and, before long, they had a comfortable relationship. Anne shared with Elizabeth her own story of being a widow in this house and raising a son by herself. Elizabeth's husband had died suddenly as well, so they could understand each other's specific pain.

Moving became a whole different story for Anne. She was delighted to leave her home to Elizabeth and her young son. Packing was easy from then on. She even left some of Nelson's bedroom furniture for Elizabeth to use. They remain in touch to this day. Anne was happy to turn over her home to her new friend. It made her own transition easier.

Claiming Your Space

Evelyn's Story

Evelyn wanted a Feng Shui appointment because her house didn't feel right, even though she and her husband Arnie had lived there for seven years. Despite her husband's objections, she paid for the consultation out of her own money. She wanted it as a present to herself on her birthday.

I began by asking her the history of the house. There could be some impact from previous owners. Arnie and his first wife had built the house together and lived there for ten years until she died. After her death, Arnie kept the house and lived by himself until he got married to Evelyn.

Evelyn's first husband died fifteen years before, and during that time she had a small apartment. After the wedding, it seemed practical for Evelyn to move into Arnie's house. It was bigger than her apartment, almost paid for, and easier than trying to buy another house.

Because Arnie had a full house of furniture, kitchen supplies, and linens, he figured Evelyn would be delighted to get rid of all of her things. She did so. So she moved in with only a few treasures of her own and her clothes. But once she started living in the house, she couldn't figure out what was wrong. She felt exhausted, tired, even depressed. She couldn't imagine what was wrong.

We walked through the house. Everything I asked about (a piano, a particular painting, an antique), Evelyn would share that it had belonged to Arnie or Arnie's wife. Finally, I asked her to show me what was hers. She took me to a small upholstered chair in the bedroom. The chair had been her mother's and Evelyn loved it. There were actually two matching chairs, but since there was only room for one, the other chair was in the basement. She also showed me a painting she bought many years ago which she absolutely loved. It was in the guest bathroom.

I looked at this sweet woman and said, "Evelyn, you're living in another woman's house." Evelyn listened but said nothing. Tears welled up in her eyes. "You're a visitor in your own house," I continued. We sat down to discuss her options.

She assured me that she and Arnie had recently discussed selling the house in order to buy some property together. Arnie was cautious about their finances and convinced her that staying there was the best option. He didn't know why she was unhappy—and she didn't exactly know either. But he felt strongly that it was in their best interest to stay in the house.

Evelyn began to share her story with me. Over the years she managed to change some things, but not without a struggle. After she moved in as Arnie's new wife, she insisted that all pictures of him and his first wife be removed. Arnie hadn't done so earlier because his kids got upset whenever he removed the pictures. Clearly, they hadn't wanted their father to re-marry. Even after seven years Evelyn still was aware of their resentment.

Evelyn had to clear out some of Arnie's first wife's clothes that were still hanging in her closet. Arnie had just "never gotten around to it." The bed they were sleeping in was the one Arnie had purchased and shared with his first wife. The choices of paint throughout the house, the wallpaper, the carpet, were all hers. "Do you like what she did?" I asked. "They're not my taste at all," Evelyn answered. Change is hard for Arnie, she explained. Any time they had a discussion about remodeling or repainting, he resisted the mere thought of it. His kids supported his viewpoint.

There were boxes in the attic, boxes in the basement, and boxes in some of the closets. Evelyn would look in them sometimes, realize they were memories from Arnie's prior life and would close them up again. She didn't feel it would be right to throw this stuff out, so the boxes were left as they were.

Mail still came to the house addressed to Arnie and his first wife. He didn't see the importance of going through the hassle of deleting her name from postal records. Evelyn wondered what else he owned that might still have his first wife's name on it—his life insurance policy, the house deed, his will. It wasn't hard for her to realize that her discomfort was caused by her status as a visitor and by Arnie's seeming indifference to her feelings. She assured me, however, that she loved Arnie and was positive that, despite his behavior, he loved her.

Since we couldn't change Arnie, we could devise a plan for Evelyn. When I asked if she had a favorite room, she told me that there weren't many places she felt comfortable. But there was one small guest room she liked. It had a lovely view of their back garden, was hardly ever used and, in her words, was the least obnoxious room in the house. We went there to look at it.

"A lot of guests?" I asked. Just one. One of Arnie's daughters used the room between jobs. I gently introduced the idea of Evelyn claiming the room for herself. Having seen the size of the house, I knew there were several other options for her stepdaughter. The thought of it intrigued Evelyn. It was both exciting and frightening. It would necessitate taking a stand not only with Arnie but also with his daughter.

We discussed what could happen in this room. I first suggested that she remove the furniture to eliminate her feeling it was a guest room. She could then repaint it with her favorite color. The first things I wanted to see in the space were her two favorite chairs and her painting. From that point, she could decide what else might work. Evelyn didn't need to be told what she would do in the room. She was already envisioning herself reading, journaling, maybe praying. Just being alone in a space that supported her would be a big relief.

Evelyn's story slowly but steadily unfolded over the course of eighteen months. She tactfully presented the idea to Arnie, choosing just the right moment to discuss the specifics. He didn't understand, but agreed the furniture in the guest room could be removed. More importantly, he agreed to tell his daughter the next time she showed up intending to move in to adjust her expectations. Evelyn went to work. The walls were painted a beautiful blue, her favorite color. The carpet was replaced. The two chairs were brought in as well as the painting. Over time she added a small bookcase, a lamp, and some plants. Every once in a while, Arnie would ask if he could join her in her special room. She gladly asked him to come in. They would have tea and discuss the back garden and other things—like his will and the deed to the house. After a few months, Arnie stood up one day and said, "I don't know what you've done in here but it sure feels good." He gave his okay when she asked if she could also redo their bedroom.

At our first appointment I had told Evelyn that their bedroom would be the next priority after her own special room had been completed. She was free to move ahead now. After discussions, negotiations, tension, and compromises, the bedroom set was given away. She and Arnie purchased a new one together—one they both liked. Per my suggestion, the bed had a solid headboard symbolizing their support for one another.

The walls were repainted a golden yellow, they bought a new carpet, and a new comforter and pillows. Arnie was ecstatic about the new look. Evelyn told me that at times she was surprised when she would hold firm to what she wanted. Her pattern had always been to give in to Arnie.

Eventually they remodeled their kitchen. Arnie loved the new look she was bringing into the house and couldn't wait for her to do another room, and then another, and on and on. Evelyn grew to love the house. Her changes removed any trace of Arnie's first wife. The boxes were sorted and the contents distributed among Arnie's kids when appropriate. Much of Arnie's old life that was stored in these boxes was no longer meaningful or memorable to him. Their relationship solidified. Evelyn felt complete support from him for the first time.

On their ninth wedding anniversary, Evelyn was shocked to hear Arnie toast his spunky wife. She had considered herself anything but spunky. Somewhere along the way she had found her own voice, and she felt good about it. Obviously, more than just the house had undergone some major changes.

Matching Goals to a Space

Jennifer's Story

Jennifer called me to look at a couple of plans for a small home she was planning to build in the next few months. The house was part of a development, so she couldn't make any substantial deviations from the blueprints. Each house design was one story with an unfinished basement where the laundry would be located. Both of them also had detached garages. Jennifer was trying to decide which plan would be the better choice.

Jennifer and I sat for a while and chatted about what she was looking for in the next few years. This was her first house and, because of its size, she didn't expect to live there for years and years. It was her intention to meet someone, get married, and start a family in the near future. She also wanted to get into a company which would pay her more money as a computer software analyst. Also, a big issue for her was health, as she had been diagnosed with clinical depression a couple of years prior. This was a continual struggle for Jennifer despite the fact that she was doing many things to counteract it.

We looked at House A first to see what might be a challenge and what would be a blessing for her. I liked the position of the master bedroom in the Partnership area. It's very powerful when a room matches the energy of that area. Having a study close to the front door wasn't a problem. Jennifer was planning to decorate it so it looked like a study, but would have a foldout couch for guests.

The Health area had challenging features in House A, with the powder room in the center and the stairs going down to the basement. The toilet, sink, and bathtub are "draining" to health and the stairway sends a message of having an "up and down" status with health. Not only that, the eating area was very close to the front door, allowing the nutrition in food to be overwhelmed by the energy coming in through the door as well as enabling that good nutrition to escape out the door, depriving the occupants of good health.

Jennifer would have a missing piece in the Wealth area since that corner was currently designed as a patio. To qualify to be part of the bagua, the area must have a roof and sides, which a patio does not have. She had been thinking of having the builder enclose it, making it a three-season porch. Because of our discussion, perhaps she would enclose the patio and make it her eating area. This would move the

GREAT RM.

MASTER BDRM.

DN.

KITCHEN

STUDY

EATING AREA

ENTRY

House A

eating area away from close proximity to the front of the house. She could create a seating area near the front, even a small library. This would be a very welcome invitation to those coming in through her front door.

House B was not without some challenges as well. Having the master bedroom in the front of the house is not restful nor does it enable the owner of the house to make a strong claim to the space. The second bedroom was considerably smaller, so it wouldn't be a good option to simply have Jennifer sleep in the back bedroom and leave the original master bedroom as a guest room. The stairs going down to the basement were very evident when you entered the space. She felt it would be possible to turn them so you'd begin the descent down the stairs from the other end.

Once again, the eating area was designated close to the front door. In fact, a table would probably be in front of the line of the front door. Both of these features relate to health issues. Both plans had the fireplace in the Fame and Reputation area, which is very positive. The fire from the fireplace matches the fire represented by Fame and Reputation.

BEDROOM

GREAT ROOM

KITCHEN

MASTER BEDROOM

DN

ENTRY

EATING AREA

House B

Jennifer decided to work with House A to see if she could eliminate the missing piece. I thought she had done a nice job of incorporating the things we had discussed *(see House A-1)*. The new layout also gave her a few more square feet of living space.

The house was built in July. During the construction, I had Jennifer drop a small toy boat in the wall near her front door to represent her ship coming in. By September she was in a new job which gave her the potential of doubling her income. The study in her new house was quickly transformed into an office before the builder was done because she was going to work part-time at home in her new job.

She met a man in December at a Christmas party who became her husband the following summer. They currently live in the house together, but are searching for a much larger one to buy together. Jennifer continues to struggle with depression, but with the new, exciting things happening to her, she is better able to cope. When I last spoke to her, they had put their moving plans on hold as she was pregnant with their first child. She and her husband were waiting to move until after the baby was born.

MASTER BDRM.

DN.

STUDY

EATING AREA

ENTRY

House A-I

What Happened to Our Marriage?

Mike and Julie's Story

Mike was the one who called me about coming to their home to assess the Feng Shui of the space. He and his wife Julie had been married for three years. A year ago they had bought a starter house, moved in, and watched their relationship disintegrate day by day. They were working with a marriage therapist and had attended a couple of marriage encounter groups. Still, something wasn't right. They were thinking of moving out of the house just to save their marriage.

I could see the desperation and exhaustion on their faces when we met. They didn't know a lot about Feng Shui but couldn't explain the sudden shift in their relationship other than the possibility that something was wrong with the house. Before we began walking around, I sat with them and asked questions about the previous owners of the house. Their home was built in the 1970s, so I figured there had to have been a few owners prior to Mike and Julie.

The first thing Julie mentioned was that they had bought the house from two people who were in a process of getting divorced. During the closing on the house, the two spouses were sitting next to each other, bickering endlessly over details. That couple had lived in the space for five years.

I asked about other owners. They had heard from neighbors that, before that couple, a family had lived in the house about ten years. The wife died unexpectedly one day, leaving a husband and two small children. Going back further in time, the original owners, who had built the house, lived in it seven years before divorcing. Mike and Julie were shocked when they realized the pattern was repeating itself. They had walked into a bad situation, and the pattern was beginning to play itself out in their own lives.

The first thing I suggested was that we take a look in the Partnership area to see if anything seemed unusual *(see Main Floor–Original Plan)*. I had spent time with them discussing the layout of the bagua based on the front door, delineating what the various areas represented and where the areas fell in their house. Before looking at the Partnership area, I could see from the blueprint that there was a missing piece in that part of the house.

When we got to the room which held most of the Partnership energy, the door was closed. Mike said, "You're not going to go in there, are you?" I assured them I would have to open the door. Julie

UTIL. RM.

BATH

KITCHEN

UP

LIVING RM.

EATING AREA

ENTRY

Main Floor–Original Plan

told it like it was: "It's our junk room!" Sure enough, when I opened the door, I could get it only partially open; boxes and miscellaneous stuff were piled from floor to ceiling. They had no basement in which to store things, so this had become their storage area. Storage was one thing, this was something else.

I listened as they talked about this room. "It's a mess." "I hate going in there." "It scares me to think about working in that area." "It's out of control." "It's mostly useless junk we can't seem to throw away." These were similar to the words they had both used in describing their marriage earlier. It didn't take them long to realize that the principle, your space mirrors your life, applied directly to their relationship. My first advice was to clean out the room.

I also suggested that, after they finished the job, they hang a mirror on one of the walls of the missing area. Now, with all the junk in the room, they would only succeed in doubling the junk if they hung a mirror in there.

When working on a relationship, making changes in the master bedroom is also appropriate, even when the master bedroom is not in the Partnership area. We spent a good deal of time in their bedroom discussing possible options *(see Upper Floor–Original Plan)*. One of the main issues was that their bed had no headboard, which implies no support for one another. They also had a nightstand on one side of the bed. I advised two matching or similar nightstands with lamps to symbolize equality in their relationship. They also had adorned their bedroom walls with pictures of family members, parents, and grandparents. In the bedroom, pictures of Mike and/or Julie were the only images that should be present. The invasion of other people's energy diminishes the energy of an intimate partnership.

Neither Mike nor Julie had been sleeping well since they moved in, contributing to their short-tempered quarrels. Even though the front bedroom was bigger, I suggested they move to the back bedroom, or at least give it a try. It would afford them more privacy and possibly less noise from the street. I was also concerned about the poison arrow coming from a corner by the entrance to the bedroom. The energy from that corner was shooting across the room and onto the bed. The back bedroom didn't have that problem. Mike and Julie said they'd consider such a move. In the meantime they could work on getting a headboard and nightstands.

Two months later, Julie called to say she was sending pictures of the Partnership room—before and after. She and Mike had noticed

Upper Floor–Original Plan

some easing of the tension between them. They were continuing with counseling and had experienced some major breakthroughs. She was most excited about what had happened to the Partnership area of their home *(see Main Floor–Original Plan)*.

She explained she and Mike had tackled the room the weekend after the consultation. They went through stuff from their college years, wedding presents they didn't need, broken chairs, and old clothes. Ninety percent of the items they couldn't use. They began throwing out or giving away stuff until all they were left with was a small pile of treasures which had meaning for them. These treasures were easily incorporated into other parts of their house. To their surprise they were able to accomplish this daunting task without a single argument or any bickering. And in the end they were left with an empty room!

They decided to incorporate the Feng Shui color appropriate to the Partnership area—pink. Since they weren't wild about straight pink, they painted the room a dusty rose—a color they both loved and that would wear well as time went by. Mike's mother gave them an Oriental rug which they put over the hardwood floor. They didn't have the money to buy a lot of furniture, so they had piles of pillows until

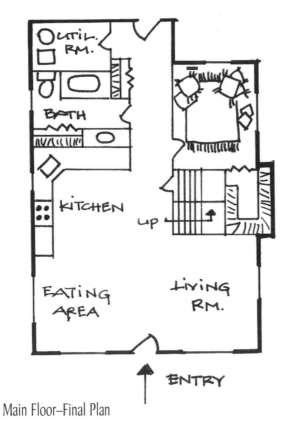

UTIL. RM.

BATH

KITCHEN

EATING AREA

UP

LIVING RM.

ENTRY

Main Floor–Final Plan

something else came along. Mike, who was in the lighting business, brought home a discontinued line of sconces which he installed in four parts of the room. The lighting gave the room a soft, romantic glow. Julie told me they had hung a mirror to increase the Partnership area of the house. The more she shared their adventures with the room the more excited she became.

She and Mike used the room as a "Partner" room. They would go in there to talk, have a glass of wine, or process some part of their therapy. Sometimes they would go in there simply to think or read. The room had become a symbol of something very important. And it seemed to be having a positive impact on their marriage.

They had moved their bedroom to the back of the house *(see Upper Floor–Final Plan)*. They were both surprised at the difference it made in the quality of their sleep. It didn't matter that the room was slightly smaller than the one they had previously used. Before they moved their furniture into that back bedroom, they decided to paint the walls a deep taupe to get away from the very white walls in the rest of the house. Mike made a headboard and they found another nightstand. They removed all the photographs of other people and hung photos of the two of them together. The photos reminded them of particularly

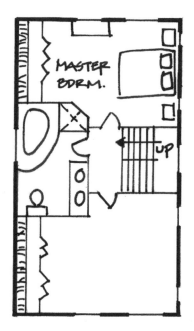

Upper Floor–Final Plan

magical and loving moments in their lives together. Julie assured me that the bedroom was now her favorite room. She had left it simple and liked it that way.

Two-and-a-half years later, I am happy to report they are still together. They continued with counseling and worked on their own issues for another year or so. They were both clear that their intention was to make theirs a solid and long-lasting marriage. I was deeply touched when I recently received an announcement of the birth of a baby girl.

Looking to the Future

It was one of those dreary Fall Friday afternoons. I had immersed myself in a blueprint a client had sent me. By 3:00 PM, as my phone hadn't rung for a couple of hours, I realized that everyone I knew must be hanging it up for the week. Around 4:00, when the phone did ring, I expected it to be a friend or my husband. Instead, I heard a male voice identifying himself as Paul. He had been reading about Feng Shui and wanted some specific information as to what it is and where it came from. I pulled myself out of my Friday lethargy and began a conversation with an intense man who, despite it being the end of the week, wanted to begin a new journey in his life.

Paul and I talked for nearly thirty minutes about Feng Shui in general and how it works. Finally, he asked if I'd ever consider doing an appointment in an efficiency apartment since that's where life found him right now. Contrary to the reaction of his friends and family, he was enjoying the experience and was in no hurry to move to a bigger place. We set up an appointment for a few weeks later.

Paul was a veterinarian. He owned the building where he worked and had created a small apartment in the back. Although he was in his mid-40s, he had just graduated from veterinary school with a huge debt load. The building where he worked and lived was very convenient and inexpensive.

When I got there, Dr. Paul was just returning a Golden Lab to its owner. He took me through his clinic, past a room filled with dogs in various stages of recuperation, an examining room, and a storage area. Suddenly, we were in his private space. It took me by surprise. There was no preparation, no transition between work space and living space. A door opened and we were there.

It was simply furnished, definitely small, and set up for extreme function. There were no frills. We sat at his kitchen table while he told me why he wanted a Feng Shui appointment. He had bought the building years ago and had a retail business of some sort lease it from him year after year. When he was ready to set up his veterinary business, he didn't renew the tenant's lease and claimed the building for himself.

He gutted the whole space to make an apartment for himself as well as space for his practice. With financial help from his cousin, he was able to change the place to the way he wanted. The business was doing quite well. After the first six months he could afford to hire an assistant to help with the phones and customers. He wasn't interested in a relationship at this time in his life and the money seemed to be going all right. So why was I here? Two months ago he was diagnosed with colon cancer. His doctor thought the cancer was in early stages and with some aggressive treatment they felt they could arrest it. The dilemma was that Paul didn't want to treat his disease with traditional medicine. Instead he wanted to use alternative methods.

He adopted a macrobiotic diet, was practicing qigong, using an acupuncturist, and having weekly hands-on healing sessions. Now he wanted to see if Feng Shui could address any issues which were present in his space. Obviously his intention was to heal himself. Since the diagnosis had been recent, it was too soon to tell if his methods of treatment were helping him, but he was convinced he was on the right path.

Because Paul owned the building, I needed to look at his living space and also the impact of the entire building. I had to assess the total picture. We began in his living space. He had been truly clever—everything was in miniature, yet workable. It was set up effectively for a single person.

When we isolated the layout of his apartment, it became obvious that he was living in a cleaver-shaped space—and sleeping on the knife edge of that cleaver. A knife edge implies cutting and slicing, a possible connection to surgery, the treatment Paul was attempting to avoid. Because he owned the building, there were some aspects of his personal life which spilled over into the business. For instance, he paid all his bills and did his correspondence in the front of his office where there was a computer. He had no television in his apartment, but there was a small one in the conference / lunch room which he'd occasionally use to watch something special.

His living space was mainly for eating and sleeping. Due to his macrobiotic diet, Paul was concerned about the kitchen and wanted to make sure there weren't any problems from my perspective. He had not been sleeping well lately but attributed this to his concerns about his health. The plumbing in the building was the one thing he hadn't redone during the massive remodeling. Sometimes the toilet made noises all night long which kept him from getting a good night's sleep.

I suggested that Paul try to keep the kitchen counters as clean as possible. He had plenty of cupboard space, but there were many items scattered on the counters. By keeping these areas clean, he would give himself the ongoing message that the food he was preparing was wholesome. I suggested a smaller table for the center of the kitchen, instead of the oversized one he had crowded in there. I also suggested that, when he ate at the table, he sit in a chair facing the entry, so he would feel strong and secure at all times.

Paul also had a closet corner pointing toward the table and the food preparation area. As the poison arrow projected energy that was too strong for a dining area, it could undermine his feelings of health and well-being. I suggested that he hang a crystal from the ceiling in front of the corner to provide a barricade for himself. I also suggested that he keep the bathroom door closed at all times. It was too close to the kitchen where food was being prepared and eaten. He didn't have any problem with that.

Since I didn't want him sleeping with his head on the knife edge, I suggested he move the futon to the other wall in the room. I strongly encouraged him to fold it up each morning to give him more space and also a sense of order. Because the space was small, I tried to impart to him the importance of keeping things in their place. Although he lived alone, there was no excuse for his clothes strewn all over the room, for his unmade bed, for the stuff all over the counter.

PAUL'S APT.

LUNCH RM.

KENNELS

EXAM RM.

RECEPTION

ENTRY

It was obvious that a second person would have a very difficult time living in this space.

I also suggested that Paul create some way to identify that he was entering his space, a space that was different from the clinic. I suggested he paint the door a different color from the other doors, or at least have a small brass sign with "Private" engraved on it. He didn't see the point, but agreed to do it. I was trying to help him find a balance between his personal and public life. As it was, business things were in his living area and personal things were in the office.

When we walked into the clinic, Paul lamented that he hadn't thought about current issues when he remodeled the building. He was presently in need of another veterinarian, but had no room for one. In order for him to expand, he would have to sell the building and move. He found himself working 70 to 80 hours a week and didn't know how he would manage if his cancer progressed.

I commended him on the rounded edge of the countertop as it prevented a poison arrow from shooting into the small waiting area he had in the front of the office. I also assured him that having a slanted door in a business was very good luck, and I wasn't surprised he was so busy. We located the center of the building where Health is reflected in the whole space. It was located in the kennel room. Unknowingly, Paul had positioned a wall running through the middle. On one side we had the exam/operating room and on the other side he had the storage and kennels. I suggested a painting be hung on the wall closest to the center, one he was particularly inspired by, one that possibly had some yellow or gold tones, since that's the color representing the Health area.

The front area was a little chaotic. Some boxes of dog food had been delivered and not put away. Paul confessed that they'd been sitting there for two weeks. One of the chair seats had been torn by a frantic puppy. I suggested that it be repaired and that the front door be adjusted so it would be easier to open. When I arrived for my appointment, I had to push against it with my back. If I'd had a squirmy dog in my arms, I would not have enjoyed that experience.

We sat in the front of the building for a while and he shared his views about his business, his personal life, and his cancer. It seems his father, an uncle, and his grandfather had all died at fifty-one. Paul was forty-nine. The cancer seemed to have arrived right on time. Although they had died from different causes, Paul couldn't help but see a pattern. Suddenly something began to fall into place for me. I had been unable to put words to my feelings, but here it was: Paul had been preparing for his departure for several years. I told him so, but he didn't get my point.

Here was a man, two years away from what he suspected would be his death, working in a space where there was no room to move into the future with another vet, and living in a space where there was no room for a future relationship. He had set up the dead end unknowingly of course. He looked at me as though I were crazy. "You need to make room for a future," I said. "I don't have room," he quickly threw back at me. "You'll need to find another place to live, use that space for another veterinarian, and move forward." I can't remember being that direct with a client before, but I could see no alternative.

I suggested that he still do the things we had discussed, but I strongly encouraged him to consider the possibility of moving. I left him with lots to ponder and hoped he would keep me posted.

Paul did keep me involved through his whole process: I helped him select another apartment, and set it up with Feng Shui principles in mind. I also helped him remodel the clinic to accommodate another vet. I even ran a Chinese horoscope for him and the new vet to check their compatibility.

Paul agreed to traditional medical treatments when he felt his health was beginning to falter. But for the most part he managed his own health care. He continues to do well and is very optimistic for the future. He loves his work now that he's not overwhelmed by it. He began dating a woman he knew from his college years and she proved to be a great support to him during some difficult moments. He is now fifty-two years old and has crossed a huge landmark. His cancer is in remission and he is planning for next year—and the next, and so on.

Getting Clear about a Partnership

Allison's Story

Allison and I were on the telephone for a few brief minutes to arrange a consultation. Yet, during those few moments, she told me what she knew about Feng Shui, the history of her house, what she did for a living, and the reason she wanted an appointment. Her main goal was to find a marriage partner. I was to find out later that acting quickly and having high expectations were standard for Allison.

Four days before our appointment, Allison called me to say that she had to go out of town on business and wouldn't be getting back in time. We rescheduled for another time in a couple of weeks. Four days before that appointment, Allison called again to reschedule. The third time she had to cancel due to business. I wondered how this woman would ever find time to nurture a relationship. I needed only two hours of her time, whereas a serious relationship would require a lot more. From our brief conversations, however, I could tell Allison was a woman who knew what she wanted.

When I finally got to her place, she was anxious to get me started on her relationship issues. Her house was a beautifully renovated lake cabin she had owned for three to four years. During that time Allison had gutted and remodeled the entire inside as well as redone the land-scaping leading down to the lake. The remodeling was impeccably done with charming details that hinted at the money she had invested in the work. It was clear that Allison had spared no expense in getting the place the way she wanted it. In fact, she told me that she had hired and fired two contractors before the third one finally followed her instructions. The results were definitely worth it.

She and I walked through her main floor. I gave her a few sugges-tions about some miscellaneous adjustments she could do to enhance the flow even more. Allison was furiously taking notes. At this point she said something that triggered some doubts in my mind. How open was she? Was she willing to fit another person into her life? I suggested she place a plant in her Wealth area to assure herself of continued abundance and prosperity. "No time to water a plant," she quipped, writing hastily all the while. She kept on moving down the hall. I didn't have a quick comeback, so I followed her to the next room. It was hard to argue with someone whose mind was so focused.

The Partnership area of the house happened to be in her bedroom. Like the rest of her house, this was a breathtaking room. I explained that having her bedroom in the Partnership area was very auspicious. I

GARAGE

EATING AREA

MASTER BEDRM.

KITCHEN

LAUND.

BEDRM.

LIVING RM.

ENTRY

OFFICE

also explained that a traditional adjustment to call in a relationship was to hang a wind chime in the room. I assured her that, from the number of weddings I have attended, this adjustment has a good track record. The metaphor behind the wind chime was to "ring in" a partner, similar to a dinner bell calling people in for dinner. Allison stopped writing and looked at me. "You've got to be kidding," she said. "Who on earth ever heard of hanging a wind chime inside the house? They belong outside. That's why they're called wind chimes. Get it? They need wind. How's that chime ever going to ring without wind?" I jumped in: "You could ring it." She looked me straight in the eyes for a moment. I thought she might actually be considering it. Her "forget it" ended any hope of that happening.

I regrouped. "The color associated with the Partnership area is pink," I began. "I hate pink." She cut me off mid-sentence. I regrouped. I pointed out that one of her bedroom windows was facing east. Hanging a round, faceted crystal in the window would catch sunlight, spreading rainbows of light and color all over her bedroom. It would be a symbol of the energy moving and changing. She stopped writing again. I thought she might actually like the idea. "It sounds too New Age-y for me." I was going to suggest placing a plant in her room to symbolize growing a healthy and vital partnership. But based on her prior reaction, I knew it wouldn't work.

I regrouped in the only way I knew how. I turned to Allison and asked her what would symbolize a new relationship to her, since obviously my suggestions weren't succeeding. Whatever she chose, it needed to be something she loved to see. It could be big or small— bigger did not always mean better.

After giving this a moment's thought, Allison headed towards her china cabinet. She carefully removed a beautiful ceramic angel which measured about eight to nine inches high. She had bought it recently on a trip to Germany. The angel held a horn which Allison likened to a wind chime. Plus it was sporting a pink sash. I assured her that both elements were important and could support her partnership intentions. She was delighted. I was relieved.

The angel took its place on her nightstand with the intention of incorporating a partner into her life. I delicately reminded her how many times we had had to set an appointment before she was able to keep her commitment with me. I reminded her of her negative reactions to every suggestion I had made, indicative of a resistance to change. She assured me that, if the right partner came along, she could and would make the appropriate changes in her life.

I took my leave of Allison, her impeccable little cabin, and her angel bravely standing in the Partnership area. Two weeks passed when I got a call from her. She was agitated and frustrated. She had come to the conclusion that the angel wasn't doing its job. She hadn't met a single prospect and was planning on taking the angel out of her bedroom. She wanted a partner and wanted him now. I strongly encouraged—insisted even—that she leave the angel in place. I talked about timing and allowing events to unfold in their right order. It wasn't what Allison wanted to hear, but she promised to let the angel do its job. "Patience is not my strong suit," she said. Oh really!

Six months passed before I saw Allison again. We ran into one another at a social event. Naturally, I was curious as to what had happened. Allison was quick to tell me her story. It seems she met a man shortly after our last phone conversation, when she was questioning the purpose of the angel. She met him on one of her business trips, enjoyed his company, and spent some memorable times with him. A few weeks later, she met another man on a different business trip, enjoyed his company, and had some memorable times with him as well. Life got complicated when she met a third man, this time in her hometown. She enjoyed him as well.

In typical Allison fashion, she juggled these three men for several months to see if there was one who appealed to her the most. She managed to keep these men secret from each other, but it took a lot of effort on her part. She would see one for breakfast in one city, fly to another city and meet someone else for dinner. They would call at different times through the week. She had to be conscious of whom she was talking to so she wouldn't call someone by the wrong name. She was hoping one of the men would be an obvious choice for her. They all began to demand more and more of her time and energy, until one day she had to make a decision.

Allison came to the realization how much time, energy, and effort it takes to be in a relationship. Even if she were seeing only one of these three men, it would require more than she was willing to give right now. Although she enjoyed their company, it was becoming obvious that none of these men was the right one for her. She broke it off with all three men and resumed her life as a single woman. She admitted to me how much she really liked her life and her freedom but hadn't realized it. In fact, she became so convinced of her decision that she returned the angel to its place in the cabinet. She enjoyed her new peace and quiet, and the amount of time she now had. She had badly missed it all.

As she was telling her story, I was thinking how beautifully and gently Feng Shui can move a person to perfect clarity. Although it seemed perfectly clear to me that Allison wasn't open to begin a relationship, she went through her own process to discover it for herself. She seemed more relaxed and centered than she had during our prior conversations.

Should I by chance relish this moment of self-gratitude too long, Allison brought me back to earth. She smiled, patted my arm, and said, "Too bad this Feng Shui of yours didn't work. Oh well, you tried." She turned and hurried off.

Picking Up the Pieces

Wayne's Story

Wayne had never heard of Feng Shui until a friend dragged him to hear me talk. He was smitten by the concepts of Feng Shui and wanted me to come to his townhouse as soon as possible.

I didn't know what his feverish excitement was about until I got to his place. Five years earlier, Wayne and his wife had bought a townhouse as their dream home. She found out later she had cancer and struggled with it for two years until she died. He was able to come to terms with her death, but was trying to find out how he to move on to a new life.

The townhouse had a garage that protruded out in front, partially blocking the view of the front door. The master bedroom was situated over the garage. The living room and kitchen were on one level, but the bedrooms were on another level. Furthermore, when you entered through the front door, you were met by a split entry. Red flags were going off all around me.

Having a master bedroom in front of the front door sets up a pattern of separation between a couple. This separation might be the result of divorce or travel, maybe illness when one of the partners is in the hospital a lot—or death. A couple must struggle to stay together when they're sleeping so far forward in the space. Added to that is the fact that they were sleeping over a garage.

This situation does not give a couple enough support to maintain a solid relationship. There can be feelings of betrayal or abandonment between them. It doesn't feel safe to sleep over a large unsupported space. If one of the partners has a tendency or potential for illness (physical, mental, or emotional), sleeping above a garage provides a stimulus for bringing that weakness into reality, as it did for Wayne's wife.

Furthermore, a split entrance with its up-and-down staircase positioned by the front door is another pronouncement of health challenges. Wayne was surprised when I asked if his wife had died of breast or lung cancer. It seems it had started in her lungs but metastasized to her breast. A split entry often hits the person entering in the chest. Wayne protested that she always entered the house from the garage—she never used the front door. The pattern for this kind of health challenge was still present.

Another staircase in the center of the house reinforced the instability of general health. And the position of the bed, the footboard pointing out the bedroom door and down the hall, contributed to

BALCONY

LIVING
ROOM

EATING
AREA

MAIN
LEVEL

UP

KITCHEN

UP

STUDY

ENTRY

UPPER
LEVEL

MASTER BEDROOM

health challenges. The "feet out the door" or "feet first" situation can imply death. The Chinese remove persons who have died in their home feet first to help them get on the right path in their next journey. This is not auspicious for people who are living.

Wayne assured me of two things: his own health was fine and he would like to stay in the space. He might want to remarry some day. He had just begun dating again. Yet his late wife's presence was felt everywhere. Her picture appeared in every room. She had collected antiques, so the house was full of her treasures. Wayne hadn't moved anything or gotten rid of anything since her death.

Wayne listened to all I had to say. I assured him we could treat each situation with an adjustment so the energy would shift. A round, faceted crystal in the center of the townhouse would stabilize the whole health area (●). Round shapes bring balance and harmony where there is unevenness. In fact, I suggested this as a priority. He could also hang another round, faceted crystal from the light fixture in the front entry to diminish the effects of the split stairs (●). We found a place to hang a mirror to energetically move the bedroom to the back of the house so it would not be so vulnerable to the street. I was suggesting a re-positioning of the bed, when Wayne said, "Maybe it'd be easier if I moved. I've been thinking about it. It might be the only way I can move on."

I could feel the wrenching courage it took for him to come to this conclusion. He understood that the townhouse didn't cause his wife's cancer. It simply provided numerous ways for it to grow. The fact that he was healthy was proof that not everyone would get sick and die in this place. But the challenge to find another house seemed as if it was more effort than he wanted to invest. But he did admit that as long as he lived here he would never be able to begin another relationship.

I discussed some "when you are ready" suggestions. When he's ready, he should replace the bed—mattress, box spring, sheets, pillows, all of it. Changing the energy in and around the bed lets go of a past intimacy to allow a new one in. When he's ready, he should make a decision about all of her antiques. He admitted that two of her sisters had asked about a few of the pieces. And finally, when he's ready, he should begin to put some of her pictures away. He needed to do these releases in his own time.

Wayne did move. It wasn't long after our appointment that he put his townhouse up for sale. I saw him at another one of my lectures. He was going to be closing on a new place within a couple of weeks so he came to pick up any new suggestions. He looked at peace, maybe relieved, maybe a little sad. Wayne told me he was keeping one antique chair he and his wife had bought together. The rest of the antiques he had sold or given away. A whole new bedroom set was being delivered to his new place the day he moved in. He still missed his wife and their life together, but it was time to move on. After my lecture I felt sad watching him leave the room. By the time I packed up my projectors and books to head home, I was melancholy, thinking that life was unfair, and that some decisions were tough. I reached my car in the parking lot and suddenly saw Wayne chatting with two women who had attended the lecture. He was expounding eloquently about his reasons for moving out of the townhouse. The two women were obviously impressed with his insights. They had just decided to stroll over to a nearby coffee shop to continue their conversation when Wayne caught my eye. He smiled and waved. It was good to see that perhaps he was indeed moving on.

Is It Time To Go?

Antoinette and I stood in the middle of her living room—or rather what would be her living room. Antoinette had lived in her three-bedroom cottage for twenty-three years, most of the time as a single parent with one daughter. She divorced her husband five years after moving in, when her daughter was three.

Antoinette had been a successful entrepreneur over the years. Though she made considerable money as a commercial real estate agent, she chose to stay in the same small home, because it provided her daughter and herself with stability. In the last couple of years, she had begun an immense remodeling program.

The first phase involved new plumbing, a new furnace, and new wiring. She was now ready to make more visible improvements. She was putting on an addition to the back of her house, providing her with a family room. She was changing one of her bedrooms into a large walk-in closet off the master bedroom. Her daughter, Jamie, was living elsewhere so Antoinette was converting that bedroom into a guest room. Plus, she was remodeling her bathroom. While all the hardwood floors were being redone on the main floor, she moved to the basement. Antoinette called me to go over her plans in case there was something more she needed to change or reconsider.

We started in her bedroom since that holds so much importance in Feng Shui. We discussed where she would situate her bed once the floors were completed. We determined there was easily enough room to put the bed in the command corner of the room. Sleeping in the corner furthest from the entrance to the room is considered a very strong, commanding spot. Being there would enable Antoinette to feel safe and secure, and she should be able to sleep better.

We also located the center of her house where Antoinette assured me she would hang a round, faceted crystal (●) for balance and harmony. The ramification of adding a family room to the back of her house happened to be a blessing. Measuring the proposed new addition, we could determine it was less than half of the full width of her home, thus making it a nice extension in the Wealth and Fame and Reputation areas. This could assure her continued success at work.

Antoinette also wanted me to see her garage where her Partnership area was located. I couldn't help but laugh when she described the area as full of dead wood. She confirmed that any attempts at igniting a new relationship in her life had not succeeded. She decided cleaning out the garage would be something she should do if she really wanted a new partner.

A year later Antoinette called me again. Things had changed. Her daughter Jamie had moved back in and Antoinette was now ready to remodel the kitchen. Even though Antoinette wanted to support her daughter, she didn't want her to get overly settled and never embark on her own journey.

The guest room was now Jamie's space. I assured Antoinette that the position of that room was a good decision since it was in the front of the house, close to the front door. These factors are conducive to moving someone along on their way.

The kitchen was being totally redesigned. Antoinette was open to rearranging the appliances to provide a better cooking experience. She was adding a dishwasher and installing all new cabinetry. She expressed her reluctance to tear up the house again but she really hated her kitchen. Her feelings were affecting her eating habits. She hardly ever cooked anymore even though it used to be one of her favorite pastimes. She either ate out or brought home takeout food.

She wanted to get back to cooking healthy meals again, since restaurant food had been dramatically affecting her weight.

Due to the small size of the kitchen, as well as the dark cabinets, flooring, and countertops, she knew the kitchen had to lighten up. Antoinette was planning to install a skylight over the stove to let some light in. I urged her to reconsider this idea, as adding a skylight to an existing building was similar to a puncture wound or a bullet hole. A skylight would bleed the energy out of her space and out of her life. Installing it above the stove would allow any nourishment from the food she was preparing to escape as well. She decided then and there to forego the skylight and instead enlarge the window over the sink.

We sketched out possible kitchen layouts. We didn't want the stovetop and the sink directly opposite one another—fire and water don't mix (the stove being fire and the sink having water energy), nor did we want the stovetop and refrigerator right next to one another (again fire—the stove, and water—the refrigerator, not mixing). Unfortunately, no matter what Antoinette did in the kitchen, it was still small. Choosing cabinets, flooring, and countertops in a lighter color was the only way she could see to expand the area.

FAMILY ROOM

KITCHEN

GARAGE

B'RM

CL.

2ND B'RM

ENTRY

LIVING ROOM

The walk-in closet off her bedroom was well-designed and efficient. Antoinette loved her bedroom and assured me she was sleeping well. Her bathroom was exquisite. She had incorporated a whirlpool tub and all new tile. In a unique way she had used glass blocks around the shower.

The family room she had added in back was her all-time favorite room. The experience of being in the room was a dramatic shift from the rest of her house. The ceilings were high and vaulted. There were large windows on two sides overlooking her backyard. A gas fireplace added a coziness to the room despite its size. A small round table enabled Antoinette to eat in there, while two big comfy chairs provided close scrutiny of the fireplace. She loved the spaciousness, the windows, the light. I was beginning to wonder why Antoinette was working so hard to make this little house work for her. Its small windows and low ceilings didn't seem to suit her style.

Antoinette shared with me that the last phase of her remodeling had gone way over budget. She had impeccable taste and had incorporated only top-quality products and first-class workmanship—down to custom drawer pulls in the bathroom and custom-mixed floor stain throughout the house. All of these options had driven the expense up considerably. Although money was not a major issue, she was still wincing from the cost of the project and was trying not to let the kitchen remodeling get out of hand.

The "dead wood" had been cleaned out of the garage. One of Antoinette's neighbors was happy to take it off her hands to use in his fireplace. However, once the wood had been removed, the floor swept and scrubbed, she saw how badly the garage floor had settled over the years. It actually sloped toward the house. This, of course, explained the mystery water that would appear in her basement on occasion. She saw this as just another major project for the future.

Six months passed before Antoinette asked me to come to her house again. As I pulled up to her house for the third time, I couldn't help but notice that from the outside the house was still small and unassuming on a street lined with similar houses. Once inside, of course, it was evident a tremendous amount of work had occurred. But from the outside, the place gave no indication of the transformation. It was still a small house.

The kitchen was now completed and her daughter had vacated the space to take a job on the East Coast. Antoinette was now considering her options for the garage. As before, when I saw the finished results of her construction, I could sense the care and deliberation with which she had chosen each and every item. The kitchen was everything she had dreamed and hoped for. The front bedroom was a lovely guest room furnished with priceless antiques which she had inherited from her family.

Antoinette had sold her share of a company. She was starting her own company at home, working off her old kitchen table in the family room. In light of that, she had decided to tear down the whole garage that was sloping and re-build a newer and slightly bigger one with an office in the back.

Antoinette made it clear she was not excited about this project—the expense and the disruption—but she felt she had no other choice. She hated how her new business was expanding all over her beautiful family room. She couldn't relax in there anymore because her work was a constant reminder. Since the room had not been set up as an office, files were everywhere. There were no provisions for storage, so things were stacked on the floor, the table, and even on the comfy chairs. To get better organized, Antoinette felt she'd have to live through one more remodeling project. By having an office in the back of the garage, she could set things up the way she wanted and get it all out of her family room. She looked tired just thinking about it.

I decided to go out on a limb. "Would it be easier for you to move?" Antoinette looked a little astonished. She admitted that she hadn't thought about it. The house had always been her domain. Leaving it frightened her. "Why don't you ask the house what you should do?" I said. I could tell from her expression she thought I was kidding. When she saw I was serious, she said, "How would that work?" I explained to her one effective way she could connect with her house would be to write it a letter. Antoinette's logical mind was struggling. "And say what? And am I supposed to believe the house would write back?" "Let's try connecting with it right now," I suggested.

"Pretend your house is a person for a moment and it is sitting in this empty chair," I said, pointing to the one empty chair around her table. "You've just told it you're going to tear down the garage and build a new one that will have an office for you. What's the first thing the house would say to you?"

Antoinette exploded without a moment's hesitation: "What are you? Stupid? Stop trying to make me into a Cadillac when I'm just a little Pinto. I'll never be what you want. You've outgrown me. You outgrew me years ago. I will never live up to your expectations. I've appreciated what you've done for me, but you need to move, girl. You'll be happier and I'll be happier. All these remodeling projects are as tiring for me as they are for you."

Antoinette stopped. She had tears in her eyes. She sat quietly for a few minutes, wiping her eyes. "Is this for real?" I assured her it was more than real. Her answers were from her heart, not from her head. After a few minutes she asked, "Now what?"

I suggested she just be with the idea for a while. Let the garage project rest and see how she was feeling in a week or so. To support her clarity about this issue, we again pinpointed the center of her house. Antoinette promised she would hang a round faceted crystal in this spot. I also recommended she convert the guest room into a temporary office. This would enable her to reclaim the family room which she so loved. Because the guest room was small and had only one little window, she had never considered using it for anything but a bedroom. I suggested she look upon this shift as temporary headquarters for her office. She could still take her cordless phone or her laptop computer out to the family room so she could enjoy the view. But she would have a place for files and storage that would enable her to have a sense of order. It would also buy her some time while she considered whether or not she really wanted to move.

Antoinette called me several times to process her thoughts. She had been out looking at other places, unsure of what she was even looking for. After a couple of months, she decided moving seemed appropriate. Her daughter thought it was a great idea as well. I suggested that she write down all the features she wanted in a new space so when she went out looking at houses she could check her list. One piece of information she had never consciously acknowledged was that a yard required too much upkeep. Although she liked to garden, it wasn't a passion. This alone opened up a lot more possibilities for her; she was now considering a townhouse.

The next time I heard from Antoinette, her house was on the market. She had made an offer on a townhouse overlooking the river. It was big and spacious and light! It had the features she was trying to create in her small house. I wasn't surprised her house sold quickly. Before she moved, I returned one final time to do a closing ceremony with Antoinette. It felt important that, after all these years, she spend some time expressing gratitude to the house for its security and shelter. We spent an hour together one afternoon while she told me her memories. Some were nostalgic and a little sad, some were happy and touching. She wanted to leave the home clear of any negativity for the young couple who was moving in and expecting their first baby in a few months.

Antoinette had me come to her new townhouse after she had become settled. It goes without saying she looked like a different person. She now had room to blossom and expand. She was cooking again for herself and for her friends. A new relationship seemed to be in the works.

A few months after Antoinette moved, I received a call from a couple who wanted me to come and look at their home. It seems that Antoinette had given them my name and number. You guessed it—they were living in Antoinette's old house. And thus we began all over again.

Creating Abundance

Jeff and Rita's Story

A dear friend called me to ask if I would help out a couple she knew from her church. Jeff and Rita had fallen on some desperate times, had no money, and were forced to move into subsidized housing. My friend wanted to give them a Feng Shui appointment as a gift.

I'm always cautious about gift certificates because sometimes the recipient doesn't quite know what to do with a two-hour Feng Shui gift. I asked if I could speak to Jeff or Rita first to get a feel for their interest in Feng Shui. A brief phone conversation with Rita allayed any concern or hesitation I may have had about going to their apartment, so we set up a time.

Their apartment was on the fifth floor of an eight-story building. It was modestly, yet nicely, furnished, but I could see some challenging structural issues from the minute I walked in. When Rita opened the door to let me in, we had to do this awkward dance around the door. There was a blocking wall so intrusive to the entry space that there was no room to comfortably enter their apartment. She graciously took my coat and led me into the living room.

Jeff was not working due to a bad back. It was his intention to return to the work world, but he needed to do some kind of retraining first. Before that could happen, he had to get well. Rita had been laid off her job as a graphic artist due to lack of work. She was not computer literate, so any future for her in this field would require additional schooling. Until they could afford that she was trying to pick up some temporary work. Added to this was an unpaid loan made a few years ago to a relative who clearly was not going to live up to a repayment plan. Their combined unemployment checks didn't meet their financial obligations, so they were forced to move into government subsidized housing to make ends meet.

One of the first things I wanted to look at was that wall that blocked the entrance. The space was so tight the door just barely cleared the wall. Furthermore, when the door swung open, it aimed you towards the bathroom. If you wanted to get into the living room, you had to close the door first to get around it. Besides that, on the other side of the blocking wall was the mechanical/storage room. Their furnace was situated so it ended up in the Health area of their apartment. The restriction of the door was in the Career area.

KITCHEN

BDRM.

F

STOR.

ENTRY

Now these were challenges I'd seen before, so I quickly and automatically began to list the common adjustments for a blocking wall, a door that opens the wrong way, a furnace in Health, etc., etc. What I wasn't expecting was their direct responses to me about each of the items I suggested—"We can't afford to do that." Jeff and Rita were very sincere in following the energetic flow of my Feng Shui logic, and they strongly wanted to get out of this spot, but they literally had no money. Buying even the smallest mirror was not going to happen. I needed to re-group.

I explained to them the idea of a mirror on the blocking wall was to give a sense of space, so the wall didn't feel so close to the door. But perhaps they might have a painting, a poster, a picture of something which had a dimensional feel to it? Something which would give the illusion of space? No, they didn't have anything like that. A travel poster? No, not that either. Rita said, "Gee, on my last job as a graphic artist, I hand-painted a garden scene as a mural for a client. Too bad, I don't have a picture of that." I pounced. "Do you have some of your paints here?" "All of them, why?" Before I could answer, she figured it out—she could paint the garden scene right on the wall. Her eyes lit up. She began to describe the scene in great detail to Jeff—the birds, the fountain, a little bench. In their enthusiasm, I reminded them that their intention was to make "an opening" or "an expansion" for both of them to allow the energy of new and productive careers to enter their lives. I had to drag them away from the wall before I lost them in the excitement of the mural—there was a lot more to look at.

To avoid the energy from going "down the drain" in the bathroom, I suggested keeping the door to the bathroom closed. That wasn't going to work because there was no fan in there and they were both concerned that it would get stuffy. We agreed they would close the door partially to minimize the impact of the toilet, but let it be open wide enough to allow air circulation. The close proximity of the bathroom to the front door sets up the potential for health problems. It seemed to me they didn't need anything more like that in their lives.

Another health issue was having the furnace in the center of their space. The potential for "burn out" is high with this situation. Typically, you place a small mirror on the top of the furnace face down to keep the fire in check (mirrors being water elements). We had to get water in there in some other way without them having to purchase a mirror. As soon as I said water Jeff suggested that they set a bowl of water on the furnace; each day one of them could check it to see that the water hadn't dried up. Rita pulled out a ceramic bowl they had bought years ago at an art fair. The earth element of the bowl would also decrease the energy of the fiery furnace. They found a place to set it where it wouldn't get too hot and filled it up while I was still there.

Due to their situation, it seemed critical to look in their Wealth area for ways to enhance their income. This happened to be in the kitchen/dining area. All I needed to do was look at the condition of the kitchen to know there might be a problem in the area of making money. I couldn't help but wonder if all the apartments in this subsidized building were set up the same way, limiting people in career advancement, burning out their health, and now taking money from their lives. It made me wonder how any of these tenants would be able to get out of their situations and move ahead in life.

The kitchen was by far the most dilapidated part of their apartment. The cupboards needed painting, the linoleum on the floor was chipped, and the faucet was leaking. They had no response from the landlord about any of their requests to improve this area. I explained the metaphor about leaking money going down the drain just as the drips of water were draining away from the water tap.

Jeff decided he'd approach the landlord to provide some paint with which to paint the cupboards themselves. Since the cupboards were dark brown, he was going to see if he could paint them white to lighten up the kitchen. Rita was eager to explore the possibilities of painting some designs on the cupboards. I explained the connection of the color purple with Wealth, so she promised she'd consider adding some purple to whatever she did. Jeff was quite sure his brother could fix the faucet for them. With regard to the linoleum, Rita assured me they had a rug they could put over the flooring to minimize the impact of such an impoverished look. None of these things was difficult. They were kind of surprised at themselves that it hadn't occurred to them before now to take care of matters on their own. By realizing that this area reflected the state of their money, fixing up what needed to be repaired became more imminent than it had before our talk.

The other issue in the kitchen was the stove. Two of the four burners didn't work. There's a story in Chinese history which connects money, food, and fire. If a person is cooking food over a fire, the implied message is that they had some money with which to get this food. The more fires, the more food, therefore, the more money.

When burners don't work on a stove, there is money potential being missed. Again, requests to the landlord to get this repaired had fallen on deaf ears.

I knew I'd have to work with something they already owned, so I asked if they had a stainless steel kettle, or teapot, or a bowl—a wok? No to all these. I was looking for something reflective they could place on the burners which didn't work to reflect the ones which did. Jeff reminded her of a matching set of candy dishes they had received as a wedding gift years ago. It didn't take Rita long to locate the two round bowls that had been carefully packed away. She seemed reticent to set these two beautiful, expensive bowls on the stove where they could get spattered and dirty. Jeff's common sense reminded her that they weren't being appreciated where they were, so why not bring them out? They could be a reminder to them of vessels in which they could gather their money. He took it further by suggesting they put coins in the bowls to begin the money flowing into their lives. Rita was less enthusiastic about the idea, but agreed to try setting one bowl on each of the non-working burners.

There is another advantage of those bowls: when Jeff and Rita were standing at the stove, they could look in the reflection of the bowls to see anyone coming up behind them.

They didn't have much cupboard space in this little kitchen, so the countertops were pretty cluttered. I explained to them the direct correlation between horizontal spaces and creativity. Both aspects relate to "vision," both literally and figuratively. The more cluttered the countertops, the more restricted their vision. Jeff and Rita reacted with horror at the condition of their creative energy. Rita began picking up various items declaring "we don't need this" or "this is no good anymore" or "let's throw these out." Within two minutes a huge area had been cleared off the counters. I didn't want her to get involved in doing a massive cleaning job just then, but I assured her she got the idea.

I wanted to show them a poison arrow aiming right at the entrance to their bedroom. This feature was the result of the storage area in the center of their space. It was virtually thrusting energy quickly and strongly, not only into their bedroom, but also onto their bed. Both Jeff and Rita assured me they each experienced restless nights. They attributed it to worrying about their future. A poison arrow, however, can greatly exacerbate a situation. Keeping the door closed at night kept either the heat out in the winter or the air conditioning out in the summer. There was not enough room to set something in front of the corner to take the brunt of its "edge"-iness as the hall was narrow as it was. Setting something there like a plant would be in the way and most likely get knocked over.

The wall went all the way to the ceiling, so there was no ledge on which to set a trailing plant to vine its way down and over the corner. Rita asked, "What if I draped some fabric over the corner, bunching it at the top and having it drape down to the floor?" I had a hard time visualizing this, but she seemed to have something in mind. She had some sheer off-white panels she had saved to use someday.

I left them for now. We all decided that working on the front wall by the entrance would be critical to get things going for them. This would be the place for them to begin.

Four to five months passed. Jeff called me one day announcing that they were moving. He asked if I'd like to come and see what they'd done before they vacated their space. I couldn't wait to see their apartment and to hear their story.

Jeff had finished his computer training and had been hired by a company to begin the day after he graduated. The money was good and the potential was even better. Rita had been given some freelance illustration work from her past employer which paid her well. Meanwhile, they furiously worked on their apartment.

The biggest change was the experience coming into their place. Rita had outdone herself. The mural she had painted on the blocking wall was exquisite and breathtaking. It looked as though you could walk though an archway into a garden and down a flower-lined path. You could tell she was proud of her work. The landlord had found it so charming he asked that they leave it for the next tenant. I was still not prepared for what was to come.

They took me into their kitchen where I stood speechless. They had indeed painted their cupboards white. The landlord supplied them with all the materials they needed to do it right—primer, sanding equipment, paint, etc. The cupboards looked as if a professional had done them. Rita painted the handles a very pale lavender and had added small lavender and green pinstripes around the edge of each cupboard. The landlord was so impressed with what they were doing that he offered to provide them some linoleum squares to replace their flooring. With new white tiles and white cupboards, the place looked twice its size. Rita had made a lavender tablecloth for their table. I couldn't help but notice the faucet wasn't dripping and their silver bowls were overflowing with change!

Jeff and Rita were moving from the apartment to a townhouse, renting it with an option to buy. Slowly, but surely, they were getting themselves out of debt. They projected that they would be able to purchase the townhouse within eighteen months. Yet they admitted they had come to love their space and even had some regrets about leaving.

Not all things were resolved. Although they were sleeping better, Jeff was still having back trouble and experiencing sleepless nights. They never did get the money owed them from their relative, despite repeated attempts. Most importantly, however, they were able to move up and out of a space that, due to its patterns, continuously fed them a message of being blocked and penniless.

Expanding Life in a Small Space

Abby's Story

Before I knocked on Abby's apartment door, I noticed a slight tightening of the muscles in my back. The sounds of crying and shouting children were emanating from somewhere. I looked around, hoping it was coming from another apartment. But when she opened the door, I took a breath as the screams blew over me in high decibel range.

Abby seemed flustered by the behavior of her children and apologized for the disruption. She was a single mother, raising a three-year-old and a five-year-old in a two-bedroom apartment. She spent the first five minutes I was there getting the five-year-old (Jason) to watch a video and the three-year-old (Joey) to eat crackers with some juice. I was soon to learn that the peace would last only ten minutes.

Her apartment was filled with toys, trikes, and a small table and chairs. The furniture showed the typical wear and tear caused by active children. The breakfast dishes were still on the table. Both boys were in their pajamas although it was nearly 11:00 AM. Abby was dressed in sweat pants and a sweat shirt. She looked tired and was clearly overwhelmed. I asked her if this was an appropriate time for me to come. Maybe she wanted to re-schedule the appointment? She felt confident the boys would settle down, so we began.

A couple of minutes into our discussion of Feng Shui, she had to get up to fix the video for Jason. More discussion. Joey then spilled his juice all over the table and himself as well. After she got him into a new outfit and cleaned up the mess, we began again. She had to jump up repeatedly to turn down the volume on the video, and Jason would promptly turn it back up. While she tended to her children, I had an opportunity to take in the small apartment. She had a lot of furniture here—more than what was comfortable. She told me people continued to give her things—chairs, tables, lamps, and she didn't have the heart to tell them no.

Despite the interruptions, Abby wanted more than anything to get help with her life and her boys. They had moved to the apartment after her divorce. She worked part-time and brought in a little money, but mostly she relied on child support from her ex-husband. Her ex had moved out of state, so he saw the boys only briefly each summer, and Abby had no help taking care of her children. In addition, her older son had allergies and her younger son had just been tested for Attention Deficit Disorder. Each child required time and energy she didn't have.

Not only was she overwhelmed, but she also needed more money. She prayed that she and her children would get healthier. A partner would be nice, but it seemed too farfetched to think someone would be interested in her at this point in her life.

Before we began walking through the apartment, Abby had to find some other form of entertainment for the boys. Jason was bored with the video. Joey was bored with Jason. She found them some coloring books and crayons and set them up at their little table. We seemed to have a brief reprieve. She explained that she had asked a babysitter to take them for a couple hours during our appointment, but the woman had called the night before saying she was sick and wouldn't be able to come. She couldn't find anyone else at the last minute, so she was hoping the boys would find some way to entertain themselves while we talked.

One of the first issues I wanted to address was her front door *(see Original Plan)*. For some reason she had moved a file cabinet behind the door. Whenever the door was opened, it only opened halfway. She explained that it was the only place she could find to store it. Having her door only open halfway was limiting her possibilities and opportunities. I really didn't care where she put that cabinet, I simply

BOYS' BEDRM.

MASTER BEDRM.

STOR.

KITCHEN

LIVING RM.

ENTRY

Original Plan

didn't want it behind her front door. She seemed daunted by my recommendation. It had been a huge undertaking to move the cabinet there in the first place. I knew it had to be moved. She needed the door to swing wide and welcome in all the good luck she could find.

On top of that, she had a blocked entry as the bathroom wall faced the front door head-on. I suggested a mirror be hung there.

When we moved into the living room, after stopping a screaming match between the two boys, Abby remarked that she wished she could afford new furniture. She didn't like the way the room looked and was sure new furniture would solve the issue. In response to my question about how much she entertained or how many people came to visit, she assured me that she didn't invite too many people into the apartment—perhaps her parents, her sister once in a while. I suggested she remove half the chairs she had. They were crowding her living room and weren't being used. For the most part they weren't all that attractive, and none of them matched.

The dilemma for Abby was that well-meaning people had given them to her. By getting rid of them, she felt she'd be acting ungrateful. We decided there might be space for one of them in her bedroom and possibly one of them in the boys' room. Her older boy overheard us and reacted vehemently. He didn't want anything to change in his room. She suggested that if there were a chair in his room, she could read stories to him sitting in that chair. He still didn't like it, so we assured him there would be no changes unless he wanted them. It took several minutes for him to settle down. Abby took him into his room, found a new coloring book and a new box of crayons which he threw back at her. She decided to try to carry him around with us.

In the dining room, I suggested simply removing a leaf of the table to give them more floor space. It wouldn't seem so crowded with a smaller table and fewer chairs. To enhance the Children and Creativity area of her apartment, I suggested she place pictures of her and her two boys on the china cabinet she had in the eating area. It would require a major re-shifting of assorted dishes, books, and miscellaneous items that were currently sitting there. While answering Jason's questions and tending to his needs, Abby agreed that the cabinet needed care, but couldn't imagine when she'd get enough time to do it. There was also an oversized plant alongside the cabinet which required a person to duck when entering the kitchen. It should be moved to make the flow of energy in her space easier.

She began to look overwhelmed and confused. The boys were getting on edge. And we were only one hour into the appointment. I suggested that I come back later. She had things to work on for now. She jumped at the suggestion. We both breathed a sigh of relief as I headed out the door.

Two weeks later I returned to Abby's apartment. The boys were off with their grandmother for the day. Abby looked like an entirely new person. So did her living room *(see Final Plan)*. I didn't even ask where all the chairs went. I was just glad they were gone. She had managed to put together an intimate little conversation area around the sofa, had reduced the size of the dining table, and moved the plant. The cabinet was better, but still needed some work. And she hadn't yet found a place for the file cabinet that was so steadfastly preventing her door from opening all the way. Nevertheless, she could tell herself that the differences were already huge. This time I knew we'd be able to make some headway.

We spent a fair amount of time in her bedroom. I wanted her to move her bed out of the doorway. She told me that she didn't sleep well, but wanted to be close to her boys' room. I suggested that she move the bed into the back corner where it would be in a stronger position. A power position is the back corner furthest from the entrance. From the power position, Abby could feel she was more in control of her life. She had a small missing piece in the Wealth area, and I thought we could do a couple of adjustments immediately. I suggested she move her bed into that corner at a diagonal, since the room was big enough to do so, and drape some fabric down from the ceiling to the back of her bed to conceal the corner. A corner like this produces a poison arrow, creating aggressive and confrontive energy. It's hard to sleep in that kind of energy unless some measures are taken to disguise it. Likewise, the fabric could make it seem as though the missing piece were not missing at all. Additionally, Abby didn't have a headboard, so the fabric could create a sense of backing and support. She assured me she loved the idea and would get on it right away.

In the master bathroom, the mirror above the sink was small and cracked. Each morning she would have to stoop to look in the mirror

BOYS' BEDRM.

STOR.

MASTER BEDRM.

KITCHEN

ENTRY

Final Plan

193

and each morning the reflection was telling her she wasn't whole. Abby was aghast at the thought of such a message. She had a bigger mirror somewhere in her storage closet which she promised she'd find for that wall.

I also wanted to find the center of her apartment where the Health area was located. The exact center was in the hall (●), a couple of feet in front of her bedroom door. She agreed to hang a round, faceted crystal from the ceiling to mark this spot. If there was one place in which she could facilitate some harmony and balance in her life, this would be a very strong place in which to do so. The intention of well-being could affect not only her own life, but the lives of her children.

The boys' room also needed to have the beds moved. Jason, the older son, was sleeping in the doorway, with his feet pointing out the door and down the hall. This is a health challenge. He was also sleeping on a wall shared by a toilet which is another health challenge. I suggested that both beds be moved to the other side of the room so both boys could see the door, but not be in the doorway.

In the kitchen, the stove was the biggest issue. It was at the end of the countertop with its side exposed to the eating area. Her younger son had nearly burned himself severely when he ran by the stove, hit a pot handle, and dumped boiling potatoes all over the kitchen. Abby decided to put a screen alongside the stove to protect her kids and keep the stovetop enclosed.

Another issue was the stovetop in the front half of the house. What this situation can create is an imbalance in the Health area of a person's life. The kitchen itself should be toward the back part of the house or apartment. Since moving the kitchen was not an option, I suggested a full-length mirror on the wall in the hallway leading into her bedroom. This mirror would reflect and "move" the kitchen wall into the back half of her apartment. Additionally, I always suggest that there be a full-length mirror somewhere in the home, to reflect a total and complete image of who you are. This mirror could do both jobs.

A few months later, Abby asked if I would like to stop by to see her apartment. It was summer and the boys were with their father for a couple weeks. I ran in quickly on my way to another appointment. The changes in her apartment weren't nearly as spectacular as the changes in Abby's demeanor and her life. Although the boys were still a handful, she had gotten some issues resolved around Jason's neediness and anger. She was working with a preschool psychologist and they were getting some great results. Jason was sleeping better and was becoming a big brother to Joey, by helping him dress and clean up his toys.

After this short time of doing Feng Shui adjustments, Abby told me how she loved her apartment now and was considering staying there long-term. As long as the boys were young enough and could continue to share a room, there was no need to think about moving. There was no new partner in her life, but she seemed indifferent about that issue anyway. She had moved her bed and was sleeping well. Being rested made a world of difference. Her new feeling of being centered and happy was rubbing off on her boys.

What she hadn't shared with me before was the fact that she had been on medication for depression for the last year. She was now feeling strong enough to begin the gradual process of getting off the drug. Abby was starting to feel whole again.

Working at Home Can Work

Phil and Louise's Story

Phil and Louise had recently moved into a new house, their first home together as a married couple. They were excited about their new life. They were self-employed, each operating from a home office. Louise was a freelance writer and editor. Phil ran a mail-order catalog business on the Web, selling computer parts. Both enjoyed their work—until they moved in, that is.

Immediately after buying the house and getting settled, Phil became frustrated with his job. Despite various arrangements of his office furniture, he could not find a comfortable place in which to settle. He didn't even like being in the space and would find excuses not to go into his office. A hard and diligent worker, Phil was not one to blow off business. Understandably, it was beginning to affect them financially.

Their home was near the end of a little street. Each day, sometimes many times during the day, they would drive by a sign which says "Dead End." This can become disheartening after a while. It doesn't take long to imagine you really are at the end of the road and can go no further.

Furthermore, their home was situated with the garage sticking out in front hiding the front door. I did not actually see the door until I had gotten out of my car and walked around the garage. A basic principle of Feng Shui is the front door should be prominent and obvious. When you are not able to see the door where opportunities and good luck flow into the house, these fortunate events will not enter the house. Both this hidden door as well as the dead-end message may well contribute to Phil's decline in business.

I suggested a wind chime be placed at the corner of the garage with a dual purpose in mind. First, it would keep things flowing in their lives and would negate the stagnation which can come from living on a dead-end street. Second, the wind chime would draw attention to where the door was located. I also suggested they move their address numbers from above the garage (obviously where they don't live) to the side of the garage closest to the front door. This would indicate the direction a visitor would take to get to the door. Also, it wouldn't hurt to place pots of flowers or shrubs, or lighting fixtures by the walk to attract the flow around the corner and up to the door.

Had I been involved in the actual siting of the house, I would have strongly urged that the house be built as a mirror image of what it presently was. That way the front door would be visible as someone approached, bringing the potential for more good luck.

When superimposing the bagua over the main floor, the garage required the bagua to extend out to the front of the garage. This meant there were missing pieces in the Career, Family, and Health areas, and the entire Knowledge area was challenged. I suggested a mirror in the entry to "push out" the wall.

On the main floor of their home, Louise had set up her office in one of the spare rooms. She had painted it a soft lavender color, added lots of plants as well as a fountain. They had splurged on some new office furniture for her as well. It was obvious she loved this space. Unlike Phil, Louise was busier than ever with her business. In addition to this room, Louise was also setting up another room on this floor as a sewing and craft room.

Phil's office was on the lower level. When we went downstairs, they explained they hadn't been able to afford to purchase furniture for this area, but hoped to do so in the next few years. Outside Phil's office was another large empty area intended to be their workout room when they could afford to buy the equipment. Phil's office was a small white room, with one little window. He opted not to buy any new

FiRST FLOOR

Main Floor Plan

Lower Level Plan

office furniture, outfitting his area with a hodge-podge assortment of desks, tables, and file cabinets. He had his desk in one corner of the room facing the little window which meant his back faced the door. I could see why he was uncomfortable in there.

We first discussed the layout of furniture. I explained the importance of being in a position to see the entrance. It signified a control of his life; he would not be caught off guard. I suggested moving the desk to the other side of the room and turning it around so he could see the entrance yet not be in the entrance. Phil stood in the middle of the room trying to visualize this arrangement. He seemed frustrated trying to figure it out. I heard him say under his breath he was pissed off. That clue sent me out the door to the room adjacent to Phil's office. A bathroom! The toilet was backed up to the same wall as his desk. Here was another reason to move his desk away from the wall.

Having discussed his furniture arrangement, I noticed how desolate and forlorn Phil's "journey" was whenever he came down the steps to go to work. He was in an isolated, unfriendly environment. Louise's office was directly over him, adding to his oppression.

As I pointed out these observations, Phil became more and more agitated. At this point he wasn't sure positioning his rickety pieces of furniture differently would make him feel better. We discussed the possibility of setting him up in one of the areas they hadn't claimed yet (the future family room or the future workout area) to give him more space. It would take considerable thought how to make it work and define the area. It was obvious to me that Phil and Louise were going to have to talk through some issues in private. Having looked at the reality of his situation, Phil was pacing back and forth by now.

The next day he called me to say they were considering putting the house on the market. It sounded like a drastic, knee-jerk reaction, but

Phil finally was able to admit he'd never liked the place. Louise had fallen in love with it from the minute they saw it—and he got swept along in her excitement. All the things we discussed the day before brought to light his disappointment and anger with himself for having compromised his needs. He was beginning to resent Louise and hadn't known why. He called to express gratitude for his enlightenment. At this moment he wasn't sure there was a solution for him that would work in that house. He and Louise were considering their options.

Four months later, Louise called to set up another appointment. They were still in the house. They had found a solution in a most unexpected way. Phil's mother had died suddenly, leaving his father sad and distraught in the house he and his wife had lived in for over thirty years. After several family discussions, Phil's father offered to pay for the construction of an apartment for himself in the lower level of their home. Meanwhile, Louise noticed she hardly ever used the sewing/craft room. Her interest in it had waned more than she realized. These two circumstances gave Phil the option to move his office upstairs. Louise wanted me to take a look at how Phil was setting up his office and also at their plans for the apartment.

Phil had already begun working in the office on the main floor. I didn't need to ask him how things were going business-wise—I could tell by his face and by his office. He explained the furniture wasn't actually brand new. His father had given Phil all his beautiful furniture since he would be moving out of the house and wouldn't need it anymore.

Phil and Louise had had some heart-to-heart conversations after my initial visit. She was devastated to think about leaving her dream house. Initially, it seemed they had both been so excited. But as time went on, it became evident that Louise began to have the upper hand in their relationship. She took over many of the decisions they would normally have made together. She took over most of the financial responsibilities as Phil's business declined. She took over the upper floor as well. Moving Phil upstairs put them on a more equal status in more ways than one.

Louise was agreeable to having Phil's father live in their lower level. She got along well with him and was looking forward to getting to know him better. He, too, was a writer, so she felt they had a lot in common. Because her father-in-law was in good health and self-sufficient, she wasn't concerned about him making demands on them. Besides, for six months of the year he was away in his condominium in a warmer climate. With the new apartment Phil's father was not only increasing the value of their home, but Phil and Louise were also increasing the depth of their marriage.

Re-defining a Bedroom

Denise's Story

After a series of classes and workshops, I had come to know Denise very well. For a time, her smiling face seemed to always appear in the front row. She was like a sponge taking in as much information as she could handle. She was remodeling her home, she kept telling me. One day, however, she called me. "I'm stuck. I've done a lot of Feng Shui in my house, but something is still not right. I'd like an outside opinion."

We set up a time to visit her charming, quaint two-story home. She was on a corner lot with a detached garage. Denise loved to garden, and it was evident from her yard, particularly on the walkway between the garage and the back door. Her husband had divorced her three years earlier, and she was still sad about her loss. A year afterward, she inherited a very large sum of money, enabling her to quit her job and begin an extensive remodeling project on her house. But, despite all the work, she felt as though something wasn't right.

By her front door, Denise had a blocked entry created by the front hall closet. However, she had hung a mirror on the front of the closet door. When she opened the door, I saw the most beautiful closet I have ever seen. She had wallpapered the inside walls, hung a clever little chandelier inside, and installed wire shelving. She had installed brass hooks on which to hang her wide assortment of gardening hats, yet still had a small area to hang coats. It was a remarkable use of a small closet.

About six months before, Denise had redone her kitchen and replaced the dark wood veneer cabinets typical of a house built in the 1960s with lighter-colored ones. Because she lived alone, she ate at a small 24-inch round glass table with two wire chairs by a window over-looking her backyard. If she had company, she used her larger dining room table. She had incorporated small 4-by-4-inch mirrors in the tile work on the backsplash in the kitchen. Denise had appropriately placed a couple of these little mirrors behind the stove to reflect the burners and to enable her to see movement behind her. She had also scattered a few on the wall where the missing piece in the Partnership area was located *(see Main Floor–Original Plan)*. A drop ceiling with fluorescent lighting and ceiling panels had been removed, visually expanding the room. The kitchen was one of her favorite rooms, she said.

Her bedroom was in the Wealth area of the house. This was the same room she and her ex-husband had shared. She didn't like the

MASTER BDRM.

UP

DN.

KITCHEN

PORCH

LIVING ROOM

ENTRY

Main Floor–Original Plan

room, because it reminded her of him, though she had already repainted it. The furniture was new and she had arranged the furniture differently. Yet there was still something she didn't like about it.

On the second floor *(see Second Floor–Original Plan),* there was a guest room and a home office for her to pay bills and write letters. Both rooms had been re-wallpapered; both had beautiful dormer windows with window seats. Denise loved being up there and would often sleep in the guest room. When I suggested actually moving the master bedroom up there, she strongly resisted, as there was no bathroom up there. I said no more about the idea. We stood in the current master bedroom while I watched Denise struggle with everything I suggested. She no longer even knew if she liked the changes she had recently made to the room. All she could do was repeat how it didn't feel right. I observed how her face changed when we went back upstairs. She loved everything about that space. Offhandedly, she said that she probably could bring plumbing upstairs above the current master bath. I knew that would be expensive and didn't know if she wanted to spend the money. I refrained from saying any more. A moment or two later she realized the view of the garden in a bathroom upstairs would be spectacular. She spent a moment imagining what it would be like

Second Floor—Original Plan

STOR.

STOR.

UP

GUEST
ROOM

HOME
OFFICE

when she was taking her morning bath or brushing her teeth. The view would be much better than on the first floor. I refrained again.

She told me that the guest room had a newer mattress and that was why she thought she slept better there. I refrained from responding to her. Denise's favorite color was blue, which, of course, was the dominating color in the guest room. I refrained again from talking. She admitted that she felt safer upstairs than downstairs. Refrained.

She could make the lower master bedroom into a den for the television currently in the basement, her least favorite spot in the house. Then she could possibly incorporate a piano into the master bedroom. She didn't have room for one now. She used to play the piano as a young girl and had been wanting to get back into playing, etc., etc., etc. Refrained again.

We went back down to the master bedroom. Denise walked in with new eyes, envisioning the television and a piano in the room. She scrutinized where things might fit. I let her be, but finally could no longer refrain.

"Why not?" I asked. I sensed her wrestling with questions: Is it all right to make a bedroom into something else? Aren't there rules about

UP

DN.

KITCHEN

PORCH

LIVING
ROOM

ENTRY

Main Floor–Revised Plan

doing something like that? What if she didn't like it? She finally looked at me and said, "That's it. It can't be worse than where I am now."

I felt as though that might be all she needed from me for the present. Denise called me with questions and confirmations several times while she was changing things. She gave herself permission to begin sleeping upstairs that first night.

Six months later, I was hired by one of Denise's neighbors. In her enthusiasm and excitement, Denise had told them her story. After the appointment, I walked over to Denise's house. I heard the tinkling of a piano as I approached the door. She was ecstatic showing me her "new house" *(see Main Floor–Revised Plan)* as she called it. The new den had taken shape very quickly. She had purchased an alcohol-burning fireplace for it. It required no ventilation. The small upright piano fit beautifully in the corner. Denise had changed the entrance door to a French door since she didn't need the privacy anymore.

The new bathroom on the second floor *(see Second Floor– Revised Plan)* was done in impeccable style. I expected nothing less from Denise. She had worked in her favorite blue colors. Once the decision had been made, she admitted, it felt right. She never doubted the end

Second Floor–Final Plan

MASTER BDRM.

STOR.

STOR.

HOME OFFICE

result. She was convinced that the financial investment in all the remodeling would not only pay off when she sold her house, but was already paying off because of the energy shift in the space. She absolutely loved the den and adored her upstairs bedroom.

It is not unusual to be stuck in your own space and be unable to see an option. A new pair of eyes can often expand your outlook. I refused to leave that day before Denise played "Blue Moon" for me on her piano.

New Life, New Breath

Peggy's Story

Peggy lived in the same townhouse for five years. It was small but adequate. She was married to a man twenty-five years her senior who had recently died. At the age of 82, he simply didn't wake up one morning. Peggy was concerned about whether she should have the townhouse blessed, having read somewhere that if someone dies in your house you're in big trouble.

Even before Will died, she was having asthma attacks. There were days when she couldn't breathe, and Will would have to take her to the emergency room. She gained weight and felt overwhelmed most of the time. She was beginning to wonder if there was something wrong with the place.

When we set up a time for an appointment, she was very adamant that when I got there I was not to enter through the front door. There was a side door where everyone entered and that was where I was to go. She assured me that a lot of people find it confusing, but that's how they had set up the place. Knowing what I know about front doors, I was concerned about this arrangement already.

I arrived at her townhouse and, despite her clear instructions, I still was confused about the doors. She came out of the side door and met me, saying she usually had to watch for people coming to visit so they can get directed to the right door.

I began by discussing the death of her husband. He had not been feeling well, but due to his age, Peggy hadn't been alarmed. A few days later, he had a heart attack in his sleep and died. She was grateful he didn't have to suffer. He had lived a full and productive life. They had traveled extensively during their marriage of twenty years. I suggested that if she wanted to clear the townhouse, she could do some very simple activities on her own. Or if she wanted my support, we could do it together. Taking a small bell and ringing it as she's walking through the space is one way to clear it. Holding a candle and walking through the townhouse is another way. Incense would also work. Will's death wasn't violent nor had he suffered for an extended time. A cleansing in this case might feel more like a blessing. Peggy decided that she'd love to cleanse and bless the house with a bell, but it felt like something she'd rather do on her own.

We then turned to the front door. In Feng Shui, front doors are considered the mouth of ch'i, meaning they're a passage for good luck and good fortune. When there's confusion around where the front door is located or when the door cannot be seen, these opportunities for good luck may be passing by. The front door needs to be obvious. Additionally, it should be a different color from anything else on the building. The preferred color is red or some variation of red, but any color will do as long as it's a color of choice by the owners. Peggy reminded me that she lives in a townhouse and wasn't allowed to paint her door. But she could put some pots of flowers on both sides of the door as well as a wind chime or a flag.

The bigger question was why Peggy was not using her front door in the first place, which required this awkward, confusing experience to happen to anyone who came to her place. She showed me a bookshelf sitting in front of the front door. She needed additional space, so she blocked off the front door from the inside. The door couldn't be used even if she wanted to *(see Original Plan)*.

Plus, when Peggy used the side door as her front door, the flow of ch'i or energy entered into her dining room. While eating food or having tea, the nutrition in the food can escape much too quickly out the door, leaving the people in the house with health problems. In addition, it set up additional food issues. It was a trigger for her wanting to eat whenever she walked into her house. Peggy confirmed that she had gained an enormous amount of weight since moving in. But she also assured me that she never ate at the table, but opted to eat at her coffee table while watching television. I assured her that actual use or non-use of the table didn't matter. The flow of the energy was still there.

Using the real front door would be ideal. She'd be welcomed by her living room, an appropriate greeting. There was a closet by the real front door in which to hang her coat which she didn't have by the side door. Of course, she asked where she was going to put her book case.

From the size and the amount of furniture she had, I guessed that she had moved from a much larger space. She confirmed that this was true. When she and Will moved to this townhouse, they were downsizing. Each of the bedrooms from the old house was larger, yet they had tried to move as much as they could into this small townhouse. There was no way to describe the experience of being in this crowded house.

The living room was small but that wasn't the problem. The problem was the sectional sofa, which was much too big for the space. Along with that, Peggy grew plants. Big ones. And lots of them. She

Original Plan

was intentionally trying to create a cozy jungle feel, which I assured her she really had created. But the room felt stifling. I couldn't breathe in the living room. Some of the plants were not doing well and needed pruning. Some simply needed to be removed. If that happened, the large sectional could work. I also invited her to think about removing some sections of the sofa to minimize its impact and get it to be more in scale with the size of the room.

There was a half-wall between the living room and the kitchen. The top of the half-wall was a counter space with far too many plants and bric-a-brac. She was trying to create a barrier, but neither the living room nor the kitchen was big enough to introduce a barrier. Her kitchen was a small galley with only one end open. Peggy needed light in there. I suggested a mirror behind her stovetop not only to bring in light but also to reflect what was happening behind her back. She had limited counter space, but almost every square inch was covered. No wonder she was having trouble seeing her future. Again I suggested simplicity.

Peggy used the back bedroom as a home office. She wrote letters and paid bills in this room, but otherwise didn't spend much time there. A gas fireplace was on one wall. She could turn it on if she was ever in the room for any length of time.

The front bedroom was where she slept. Peggy and Will had moved their king-sized bed into a room that could not accommodate such a large piece of furniture. The room was wall-to-wall bed. There was hardly any space to move around. One side of the bed was up against the wall. The only free corner had a huge palm tree reaching out towards the bed. A walk-in closet off this bedroom housed a dresser and an overabundance of clothes, many of them her late husband's.

At this point, Peggy and I decided to sit down to determine how she wanted to live her life now that she was alone. She told me that a life insurance settlement had left her with considerable money, but she wasn't yet ready to move. The thought of moving was scary. She simply wanted to improve the conditions in the townhouse. We discussed the fact that Feng Shui views the back of a space as private. This is where the bedrooms and the kitchen should be located. Her bedroom was in the front of the house. Was there any way she could trade her office for her bedroom?" Bring the office to the front of the townhouse and put her bed in a safe back corner. I also suggested she down-size her bed. She agreed she was ready to do that. It felt too lonely sleeping in such a large bed without Will.

To me this was a crucial place to start. Her son lived in the area and had offered to help her in any way. It seemed to me her asthma could be linked to the oversized furniture as well as the overwhelming number of plants and other items. It was no wonder she couldn't catch her breath. I strongly urged her to reconsider all the plants and determine which ones she really wanted to have in her home.

Peggy kept me posted. She and her son spent many days cleaning out and moving furniture. Peggy's asthma seemed to get progressively worse as they shuffled things around. Twice in one day he rushed her to an emergency room because she couldn't breathe. She still insisted on continuing with the project, thinking her condition was related somehow to the condition of the townhouse. I finally returned about two months after our initial visit to see what had happened. She wanted further advice.

The front door was still blocked, but the amount of work in the two bedrooms was astounding *(see Phase 1)*. Her son had painted both of the rooms. Her bedroom was a soft lavender—her favorite color. It was also appropriate, considering the bedroom was in the Wealth area of her space. She had found a double bed, which allowed the dresser from the walk-in closet to be moved into this room. Peggy had only one large plant left in the bedroom despite her inclination to move in a bunch more.

The front bedroom had been transformed into an office. Basically everything stayed as it was in the back room. The room was painted a beautiful periwinkle blue. I suggested a mirror over her gas fireplace to balance the fire and to correct the missing corner in her Knowledge area. A mirror will expand a space and "move" a wall. I also asked about changing the hinges on the closet door so it wouldn't keep bumping into the door to the room. These create an "arguing" vibration. By changing the door on the closet, she would be reflecting more harmony in her life.

Peggy had moved a fold-out couch into the room that was now her office. When I asked her who would use the couch, she realized she never had guests that would stay overnight. There was no use for it anymore. She hadn't thought about whether she should get rid of it or not. I suggested she give it away or sell it. "Funny," she commented. When she and her son were moving the fold-out couch, he had off-handedly said when she didn't want it anymore he could use it. She commented how blind she had become about her possessions. It hadn't occurred to her to let them go. By doing so, she would have a place for her bookshelves in front of the front door.

Before we left the office, she showed me the walk-in closet which had been made into a storage area. Then she showed me the closet off her bedroom. It had required sorting through clothes, memories, and treasures. During this process, Peggy had had one of the worst asthma attacks she'd ever endured. But the sorting got done and she was very relieved. In fact, in the last few weeks she'd hardly had any trouble with asthma at all.

All of this cleaning and sorting had spilled out into the living room as well. Even though there were still a lot of plants, many of them had been removed. She had given some of them to friends and neighbors. Because she never used her front door, Peggy had positioned the furniture accordingly. If she were to begin using the door, she would need to look at rearranging things. She shared with me that deep down she didn't want the television in the living room, as she couldn't overcome the temptation to watch it. She found herself overeating while staring at some program she didn't even care about. And she felt she could make better use of her time if she wasn't tempted to turn it on. We

CL.

P's B'RM

ENTRY

OFFICE

CL.

Phase 1

227

explored the possibility of removing it altogether, moving it into the office which she could make into a den, or getting a cabinet with doors on the front so that it wouldn't be so prominent in the room.

Peggy really liked the idea of putting it in a cabinet with doors. But she resonated more with moving it into the office. She could see the value in redefining the office as a den since she didn't use the desk more than an hour a week. Maybe she'd need the foldout couch after all!

The other issue Peggy wanted to discuss was her kitchen. Not much had happened there. I suggested she remove every single item, plant, and bric-a-brac off the top of the divider wall and leave it empty for nine days. I wanted her to experience it for a time. Then she could replace whatever items she thought she'd like to have there. She also wanted a further explanation of the mirror behind the stove. She wasn't sure she'd like that, watching herself cook and all. But, she had a mirror in her storage area which she brought out and propped behind the stove to see how it might look. The point of the mirror, I said, was to bring more light into the dark kitchen and to reflect the world going on behind her. She'd give it a try.

As I was leaving, she handed me a plant. I assured her I'd give it a good home. She asked for another appointment, and two months later I returned.

You can imagine my surprise and delight *(see Phase 2)* when I pulled up to Peggy's townhouse and I saw two planters of red flowers standing on either side of the new front door. The door was open and Peggy was ready to greet me when I got out of my car. She looked fabulous and I told her so. A friend of hers was taking her to an aerobics class for seniors, and she had to admit she was starting to feel better. Although she had lost no weight, she could feel a distinct difference in her body.

She had waited for me to help her arrange her living room furniture. I noticed the television was gone. She'd given it away. Every single plant had been removed, and the plants were gone from the top of the half-wall. She confided that, when the last plant was moved out, her asthma seemed to have moved out too. She was hoping to incorporate a few plants here and there but was waiting for some input from me. The most stunning change was Peggy had gotten rid of the sectional and had replaced it with a small sofa and two chairs. The furniture was perfectly scaled to the room, yet still big enough for comfort.

P's B'RM

CL.

OFFICE

ENTRY

Phase 2

Before we began moving furniture around, Peggy wanted to show me the office, which was no longer just an office. She had kept her fold-out couch and had created a cozy little space for herself. She had replaced her large desk with a smaller one. The bookshelf fit in perfectly. And in the corner was a small television for those times when she wanted to watch something. The television hardly made an impact on the room as it was small and in a little cabinet with closed doors. An Oriental rug tied the whole room together. A fountain kept the ch'i flowing. Besides her bedroom, it had become her favorite room, and I could see why.

It wasn't hard to let the furniture find its proper place in the living room. We found a couple of areas where a plant would be the perfect touch, much to Peggy's delight. I suggested a round coffee table at some point, as it would be a nice message of harmony and cooperation. I also suggested a round table in the dining area for the same reasons. Peggy had reluctantly removed all the clutter from the divider wall to discover after a couple of days she really liked the look. Things felt quieter and less hectic. She decided to put nothing back in the house. She would leave it clear of all items.

Based on the new bagua, we located the exact center of Peggy's space (●), which was in the hallway. She opted to hang a wind chime denoting this spot that she could ring as she walked back and forth in her hall. Her intention was to "call in" good health and a balanced life.

Two years later, Peggy continues to live in her townhouse. She continues to work on her tendency to clutter up her house. Her asthma remains a challenge. When her space starts to feel too stifling due to clutter, she notices that her asthma is more acute. She realizes that when her space can't breathe, neither can she. Peggy's space reflects her life.

In the two years since she began her journey with Feng Shui, she has lost over twenty pounds. As with her space and her asthma, Peggy's weight issue is a continual process. Overeating had become another form of clutter in her life.

De-cluttering an Office and More

Alice's Restaurant

After seeing her youngest child graduate from high school, inheriting some money from her family, and selling the oversized house that had seen her through a 20-year marriage and divorce, Alice turned to the one passion she had all her life—cooking. She had always dreamt of owning a small restaurant that served organic food. She took some of her money and leased a well-positioned storefront to provide the community with her outstanding culinary creations.

Alice believed in the integrity of natural, organic foods. Her cozy little restaurant was an immediate success. People came from across town to taste her homemade soups and fresh-baked bread. Her smiling face along with her friendly banter brought even more people to the door.

One of her longstanding customers asked her to cater a major charity ball. Thus was born a secondary direction, catering. It began to take more and more of her time and became the more lucrative side of her business. She would often work 16 to 18 hours if she had to cater an event in the evening. Many mornings would find her in her kitchen at 4:00 AM baking bread. She had some part-time help, but they didn't have the same passion. Alice was often singlehandedly preparing lunches and dinners for the clients who came to her restaurant, and, in between, getting food prepared for seventy-five people that evening. She had to admit, though, she was in her element.

But time began to take its toll. Passion or not, a person can keep a schedule of this intensity only for a limited amount of time. Her life became out of control. Her office was hopeless. She had no time to enjoy her financial success. She had to give her dog to one of her daughters since she was never home to care for him. It was after this heart-breaking decision that she called me.

We had to meet on a Monday because the restaurant was closed that day. Alice basically wanted to get control and balance into her life again. She loved every aspect of her business, but it had far surpassed her expectations and she couldn't keep up. Her office mirrored this situation.

It seemed most beneficial that we start assessing Alice's office since it reflected her energy more intimately than the restaurant itself. Her desk had stacks and piles of papers, mail, and canceled checks along with her computer. The floor was likewise filled with stacks of magazines, more papers, tax forms, etc., etc. A credenza was buried with boxes of samples of dinnerware and cutlery. All of this stuff spilled over onto a small round table. It was hard to know where to begin.

Because Alice spent the majority of her time at her desk, I suggested that we start there. In an area overrun with clutter, I will usually tell a client about a Feng Shui method for clearing a space which involves removing nine items a day for nine days. The number nine is an auspicious number representing success and completion. Although it doesn't seem like much of an effort on a day-by-day basis, at the end of nine days, eighty-one things have been moved, filed, tossed. The reason for doing a little each day is to build the momentum gradually. Alice was ready to move all eighty-one things that day and be done with it. Instead, by doing something around this issue each day, she would reinforce a new pattern for herself. A habit takes repetition before it sticks.

I also suggested that she hang a crystal in the middle of her office (●) to balance and gently move the energy. She could also hang it with the intention of getting guidance and clarity, and to bring in the appropriate help she needed.

Additionally, I suggested a new arrangement of furniture she could implement at some point. As it was now, her desk was too close to the

Before

After

entrance. Alice had assumed a "gatekeeper" or receptionist position which left her susceptible to too much activity. Being so close to the door, a lot of issues could easily land on her desk. My suggestion was to move the desk to the back corner to alleviate this tendency. We agreed that a lot had to be cleared out before such a move could realistically take place.

Six weeks after my visit, I drove by Alice's restaurant and noticed a "Soon To Be Closing" sign in the window. I called her at my earliest opportunity. She sounded upbeat and spirited. She'd been meaning to call me but with everything going on she hadn't had time. I expressed my regret at losing a wonderful eating establishment in the neighborhood. Alice said that as she was doing her "nine items a day for nine days" process, she began to listen to her feelings and to her heart. After the first cycle of this clearing clutter method, she began a second round, when one day she just knew what she had to do. By the time she got around to moving her office furniture, her plan was ready. Although she loved the restaurant business and enjoyed chatting with new customers, Alice saw how draining it had become to own both a restaurant and catering business. For the amount of effort and time the restaurant required, financially the returns were small.

Her catering business, however, still enabled her to meet people while she could continue to cook. From a financial standpoint, the catering side of her business would provide her with a comfortable income without all the stress. The decision to close her restaurant was obvious. She would not have the tortured schedule. She would not have the overhead the restaurant required. She would need less hired help. And, more importantly, she would have more time to devote to herself and her family. She could even get her dog back.

As with many people, Alice's life got out of control before she recognized what was happening. By one standard of measure, she was successful and could be happy. But by her own personal standards, things were not right. Shifting items in a cluttered and crowded environment can loosen up many things besides furniture and paper. It can also open up space, providing room for clarity and new possibilities.

Glossary

A

Arrows, Poison—*See* Poison Arrows.

Aquariums—Often used in an area where things feel "stuck." The gentle flow of the water and the movement of the fish can enhance money if placed in the Wealth area of the bagua. The water element of an aquarium can also offset the effects of "burn out" from a fireplace, if placed on or near the hearth. If an aquarium requires too much time to maintain, a picture of fish or a sculptural fish piece (i.e., dolphins) would also work.

B

Bagua—A mental map determining the placement of nine life issues in a home, on the lot or a garden, over a desk, or on a bed. When a bagua is appropriately placed and enhanced, your life begins to manifest good fortune and blessed occurrences. The nine areas are Career, Knowledge, Family, Wealth, Fame & Reputation, Partnership, Children & Creativity, Helpful People, and Health.

Beams—Can be divisive between a family or between business relationships. They should either be removed completely, if possible, or painted the same color as the ceiling to minimize their impact. If the beams can neither be removed nor painted, avoid sitting under a beam at your desk or in your favorite chair. And avoid lying under a beam when in bed by simply moving the bed.

Bed—One of the three most important pieces of furniture in a home. (*See* Desk and Stove.) The bed should be positioned so that it is in the command position of the bedroom. (*See* Command Position.) When lying in bed, the occupant must be able to see the entrance to the room. It is important that there be nothing stored under the bed and that there be an adequate, solid headboard on the bed. There should be sufficient space around both sides of the bed to get in and out either side, representing more options in life. The bagua can be superimposed over a bed orientating the foot of the bed as the front of the bagua. When working with the bagua on a bed, the energy or ch'i around an issue can be changed by intentionally placing items between the mattress and the box-springs of the bed.

Bedroom, Guest—The closer to the front of the house, the less likely guests will stay long. Guest rooms can serve additional functions, like being a part-time office, an exercise room or sewing room. Guest rooms can also be located in the lower level, near the front door, or over a garage without serious consequences.

Bedroom, Master—Ideally in the back of the home. The bedroom should not be over a garage, near the front door, or at the end of a long hallway. Bedroom should not be cluttered with television, computer, books, pictures of family or friends, or exercise equipment. Master bedroom should ideally be in a command position of the house. (*See* Command Position).

Bells—Can be used to "call in" an intention. Hung near a back door that falls in the Wealth area of the house, a bell can slow down the quick exit of money. A bell can be hung on a doorknob or near a front door to act as a form of protection to those who work or live there. It is important that the bell have a pleasant sound to the occupant and not be a source of irritation when it rings.

Birdbaths—See Ponds.

Blocked Entry—A wall or structure that impedes someone from walking straight ahead into a space. A mirror or a print or painting with a dimensional feeling will "open up" the space. Creating the illusion of space keeps the energy flowing.

Bookshelves—Whether at home or in an office, need to be kept in order. Shelving should ideally only be waist-high in an office so as not to feel overwhelmed when seated at a desk or in a chair. If shelves go higher than eye level, then keep the upper shelves "light." The use of plants, artwork, or photos can soften the impact of tall shelving. A library would naturally have tall book shelves, which are acceptable, yet they still need to be kept in order, with current books, eliminating out-dated information. *(See* Library.)

C

Candles—Can be used to "enlighten" a space or get "enlightenment" around an issue. The intentional lighting of a candle brings illumination, both physically and mentally.

Career—One of the nine areas of the bagua that represents the activities and directions for your pursuits in life. It is represented by the color black.

Ch'i—Universal energy. Feng Shui works with enhancing and manipulating the flow of ch'i in a space or an environment.

Children & Creativity—One of the nine areas of the bagua that includes anything which you may "birth" in life, in addition to children—a book, a thesis, poetry, music, business, etc.

Clocks—In order for your life to keep "ticking" along, all displayed clocks need to work. A malfunctioning clock can give a message that something else in life is also not working.

Clutter—Too many items in a space causing unclear thinking and feelings of overwhelm and exhaustion. Clutter can be unspecified piles of paper, magazines, newspapers, or it can be unused clothes in the closet. It can be unfinished projects, too many books or collections of items.

Colors—An option for adjusting energy in a space. Colors should be used that are liked by all members of the family or business. Each area of the bagua has a color connected to it which can be used in its pure form or any shade or tint of it:

> Career—Black
> Knowledge—Blue
> Family—Green
> Wealth—Purple
> Fame & Reputation—Red
> Partnership—Pink
> Children & Creativity—White
> Helpful People—Gray
> Health—Yellow

Command Position—Back corner of a space at the greatest angle from the entrance door. A command position establishes ownership and control in the space. It is ideal if the master bedroom can be in the command position in a house, or if a bed can be in the command position in the bedroom.

Creativity—See Children & Creativity.

Crystals—A round, faceted crystal acts as a barrier when too much ch'i comes down a hallway; it balances out distortion or unevenness; a crystal can bring about clarity and calm a sense of overwhelm. A round, faceted crystal can also infuse a space or a situation with a gentle movement where previously there was stagnation. A crystal hung in the center of a space can bring overall balance. It is more effective if the crystal is hung with a thread, string, or fishline that has been cut nine or eighteen inches long.

Cul-de-Sac—Might be a potential for stagnation and a challenge for moving ahead. A house or business that is situated in a cul-de-sac is a recipient of the "dead end" of the road's flow. There appears to be nowhere to go. A small island in the middle of the turn-around would effectively direct the flow to keep on track and not allow it to puddle in the center. But often, this is not possible, so the individual spaces could make adjustments to assure the continuance of flow and movement by installing a fountain in front of the establishment or home, by hanging a wind chime in front of the entrance, by having a spinning weather vane on top of the house or building, or by having a small, ornamental windmill by the front door.

D

Dead End—See Cul-de-Sac.

Desk—One of the three most important pieces of furniture. (*See* Bed and Stove.) The desk can hold a message of creativity and productivity or stagnation and heaviness depending on the amount of clutter stored on it. A desk would ideally be placed in the command position in an office (*see* Command Position) with the chair supported by a wall. Additionally, the desk should be positioned so that when seated at the desk, a person would easily see the entrance to the office. If there are no options in the office and a person must sit with their back to the entrance, then a small mirror positioned so that the desk's occupant can easily see behind them would be helpful. The desk should be appropriately sized to the proportion of the person using the desk. The bagua can be oriented over a desk with the front edge of the desk being the front of the bagua.

Door, Arguing—When two doors hit up against each other while trying to open or close either of them. If possible, change the hinges of one of the doors so that it opens another way to prevent the two from clashing. Arguing doors implies some argumentation in the space between those who live or work there.

Door, Back—Important to maintain the "flow" in life. A back door allows energy to come in and go out. The only problem area is if the back door falls in the Wealth area of the bagua. A wind chime either inside or outside the door will counteract money coming in the front door but going out the back door too quickly. It is important to always have a back door somewhere in the space. If there isn't one, a full-length mirror hung somewhere in the space (just not in Wealth) can represent the energy flow of a back door.

A back door should not be lined up directly with the front door as too much energy or ch'i can rush through the space. A front-door/back-door alignment indicates lost opportunities. Something physical needs to be placed between the two doors, like a screen, a plant, a round faceted crystal, curtains on the back door, a piece of furniture, etc. A back door should also not be in the Wealth area of the house as it is too easy for money to escape. Placing a bell or wind chime near a back door in Wealth can ease the rush of finances out the door.

Door, Front—Often called the "mouth of ch'i" since it is the place through which opportunities arrive into a space. A front door should be the first feature to be seen when arriving at a home or office. It helps if it's a stand-alone color and does not match shutters, trim, or shingles. If the front door is not used often due to an attached garage or a garage in the back of the house, it is advisable that the occupants or owners use the door on a regular basis to activate the ch'i around it. If the doorbell doesn't work, there is an indication that someone in the space is not being heard or acknowledged. All doorbells should work and be pleasant to hear.

Driveway—See Roads.

E

Elements—See Five Elements.

Energy—See Ch'i.

Extensions—A small protrusion from the main part of the house or room that measures less than half the full width of the space. An extension is auspicious and gives extra energy to the corresponding area of the bagua. Extensions do not need to be adjusted or changed in any way. Although the bagua does not directly include an extension in its layout, the extension is still part of the space and needs to be kept in order.

F

Fame & Reputation—One of the nine areas of the bagua representing your image and how the world sees you. It represents your integrity within the community and recognition. The color represented by this area is red.

Family—One of the nine areas of the bagua including members of your family of origin—parents, siblings, cousins and relations, as well as anyone you would consider part of your extended family. The color of the Family area is green.

Feng Shui—An ancient Chinese art of placement, literally translated as "wind" and "water."

Fireplace—Can often create too much fire, burning up the energy around health, money, or career. The fireplace can be modified by adding some water elements to its surroundings, like a fountain, an aquarium, a picture of water or a seascape above the mantel, a picture of fish or a boat, or a mirror.

Five Elements—Fire, earth, metal, water, wood. The Five Elements are phases in nature that interact in constructive or dominating cycles. These five elements make up all that exists in the Universe. How the elements interact with one another determines the balance or imbalance in nature, in our spaces, and in our lives.

Flowers—Fresh or silk flowers are appropriate. Fresh flowers need to be carefully monitored as they are already dying. As soon as they begin to wilt, it is important to remove them immediately. Silk flowers can be used as an alternative, keeping them clean and dust-free. Dried flowers should not be used as a Feng Shui adjustment at all unless they have some poignant or sensitive connection to you, like a dried wedding bouquet.

Fountains—Add water, movement, and sound to an environment. Fountains are good for getting things moving or flowing again. They need to have clear, fresh water on a regular basis along with a total clean-out once a month to keep the flow going.

Furnace—Provides too much fire when in the center of a space, causing "burn out." Placing a small mirror face down on top of the furnace or the duct work tempers the impact of the fire energy. The mirror stays there indefinitely.

G

Garages—Should be kept in order and clean. Although usually a functional place to store cars, a garage may well be part of the bagua if it is attached to the house. Keeping things in order and swept out is a good activity to do if the garage is attached. Garages are more problematic if positioned in the front of the house, blocking the attention intended for the front door. The garage doors should be the same color as the rest of the house to allow the front door more notice. Just because a garage may not be attached to the house, there is still reason to keep a detached garage in order, since it is still on the property and is storing or holding possessions in your life.

H

Headboard—Represents support for the individuals sleeping in the bed. An ideal headboard is solid and comes up higher than the pillows.

It should be attached directly to the bed frame and be sturdy enough to lean up against.

Health—One of the nine areas of the bagua representing physical, mental, emotional, and spiritual well-being. The Health area is in the middle of a space. It is the core or hub around which life revolves. It is critical that this area be addressed for overall balance in life. The color for Health is yellow.

Helpful People—One of the nine areas of the bagua representing those people who can support you emotionally or financially. They might be a best friend, a relative, a minister, a plumber, a realtor, or a travel agent. The color for Helpful People is gray.

I

Intention—The power behind Feng Shui. The power of your thoughts and of your attention will enable you to bring about changes you want in life. Thoughts are a form of energy which can be focused on any object or activity to help you magnify your intention. Any object or activity used for Feng Shui purposes works on your behalf to bring about what you want.

K

Kitchen—Should ideally be in the back of the house away from the front entrance. The health of the food or the act of eating requires privacy, otherwise the energy from the front door can overwhelm the food value and its nutrition. Ideally, the kitchen should be primarily white in color with some accent colors of choice. Keeping counter-tops clear and clutter-free can enhance health and creativity.

Knowledge—One of the nine areas of the bagua reflecting learning and education. The Knowledge area is also representative of the inner journey of self-knowledge. The color for Knowledge is blue.

L

Library—A good room to have near the front door, reinforcing the intellectual nature of the inhabitants of the house. Keep only current books, discarding those that have old or out-dated ideas.

Lighting—Can be used to create change. Good, deliberate lighting can enhance your ability to "see" more clearly and to be "enlightened" around a goal. All burnt out light bulbs need to be replaced as soon as possible, as well as any lamps or lights that don't work.

M

Mirrors—Should be clear and clean to accurately reflect your intention. Mirrors can enlarge a space, create a new space, make a wall disappear, move a wall, flatten a wall, or deflect negativity. A mirror will do what your intention has directed it to do. Any broken, chipped, cracked mirrors need to be replaced, as do mirror tiles or narrow panels of mirror, since you cannot see yourself totally.

Missing Pieces—Denote a challenge or lack in a specific area. When a piece is missing in a home or a room, there may well be a challenge in that area of the bagua. All missing pieces should be addressed to prevent any potential misfortune.

O

Oval Shapes—See Round or Oval Shapes.

P

Partnership—One of the nine areas of the bagua, representing personal partners or business partners. The color for Partnership is pink.

Pillars—Round ones preferred. Square pillars create poison arrows (*see* Poison Arrows) causing disturbance and unrest. Round pillars do not have this feature and so are more friendly and workable. Square pillars need to have vines wrapped around them or small white lights. Painted vines would also be effective. Mirrors on all four sides of the square pillar would also negate their effects.

Plants—Are suitable when there's an intention of growth or expansion around an issue. A silk plant may be appropriately substituted where a real one would not do well. Any sickly or dead plants that are being used for Feng Shui must be removed from the area in which they were positioned so they don't adversely affect the issue.

Poison Arrows—Protrusion into a room or space. The corner resulting from this protrusion directs too much hard, fast-moving energy into the space which could affect those sitting or sleeping in its path. A plant placed in front of the corner could soften its impact or a round, faceted crystal hanging from the ceiling in front of the corner could negate the effects.

Ponds—Can be advantageous in a garden to enhance the flow of money. Ponds, like birdbaths, need to be filled with fresh, clear water. Having a bubbler or fish in the pond will activate its energy even more.

Pools—See Swimming Pools.

R

Red—A favorite Chinese color. The color red can effectively be used for front doors in a residence or business. Even placing pots of red flowers near a front door can be helpful, or a wreath with silk red flowers. Being a quick-action color, it can get energy moving quickly and effectively.

Reputation—See Fame & Reputation.

Roads—Act as rivers of energy and can be supportive or challenging. A soft, meandering road or driveway approaching a house is best, for it allows the energy to get there without too much or little movement. When a road or driveway approaches a house head-on, too much energy sweeps over the house or business causing overwhelm. A "protective barrier" needs to be installed to prevent this over-activity. Trees, a hedge, or a fountain could provide the protection a person needs to safely live or work in this situation.

Round or Oval Shapes—Imply harmony, balance, cooperation and conversation. A round or oval table is the best for discussions, meetings and eating meals. Round or oval shapes in the master bedroom enhance the relationship between the couple who sleeps there. Round, faceted crystals add balanced and harmonious energy to a space.

S

Split Entry—Usually splits those entering from something in their lives—their health, their money, a partner, their children, good decisions. Split entries present two staircases immediately upon entrance into the space. One goes up (usually to a living area) and the other goes down (sometimes to a family room or to bedrooms on a lower level). There is always a moment of indecision about where to go when first entering the space. The stair-rail is usually centered in front of the entrance to provide a "splitting" assault when first entering. A round rug or a round, faceted crystal hung above the stair rail, even from an existing light fixture, can help ease this tension.

Split Level—Where people operate from different areas in life. A split level has part of the living space on one level and, after ascending or descending a few steps, another part on another level. There are sometimes as many as five various levels from which a person or a family has to operate. This situation is not conducive to unity among those who live there and unity with others outside the family. A round, faceted crystal in the center of the house will help to balance out the various levels.

Stairs—Carefully placed can be beneficial. When stairs fall in the center of a space, they set up an overall theme of "up and down" with regard to health, as well as money, career, relationships, etc. Ideally a staircase should be built with a gentle turn in it to ease the energy up the stairs. There should be no open risers. They should be well-lit and eventful as a person moves through them, with pictures, color, plants. A staircase situated directly in front of the front doorway invites money and health to exit the space. A round rug or a round, faceted crystal between the door and the bottom step can ease this flow.

Statues—Imply heaviness and are therefore appropriate when trying to anchor a situation. A large statue in the Partnership area of the back yard can help to keep a good relationship in place. A statuary image of a deity can likewise anchor a job if placed in the Career area of the space.

Stove—One of the three most important pieces of furniture. (*See* Bed and Desk.) The stove (meaning stovetop, not the oven) has the potential for enhancing money as well as for providing a sense of control in life. Ideally a stovetop should be positioned so that the cook can see the entry doors to the kitchen. When this can't happen, position a mirror so that when facing the stove-top, the cook can see movement behind them and be prepared for any interruptions. Additionally the burners should be kept clean and in working order, rotating the use of all the burners. Using only one or two burners or storing items on some of them decreases the flow of wealth and should be avoided.

Swimming Pools—Are best if kidney-shaped or rounded. The sharp corners of a pool can create a poison arrow if pointing toward the house, especially a bedroom. A pool is best positioned off the Wealth area of a house.

T

Tables—See Round or Oval Shapes.

Toilets—Can create a "drain" in life, particularly when positioned in the center of the space. Keeping the lid down on the toilet and the door closed to the bathroom can lessen the impact of the drainage. A plant (even silk) placed on the back of the toilet tank can also counteract the downward flow of energy. It is important that the plant be growing upward, not a vine trailing downward. Also a mirror hung on the outside of the bathroom door can bounce back any beneficial energy that could be flushed away.

W

Weather Vane—Can be used to activate a "dead end" or to "puncture" the energy of a poison arrow.

Wind chimes—Can be effective when wanting to "call in" a particular situation or thing or whenever the energy seems stagnant. It is important that the wind chime be pleasing to the ear. It is an effective adjustment outside the front door when counteracting the energy from living on a "dead end" street. It can also be used inside or outside a back door that is in the Wealth area of the house or business to prevent money from leaving too quickly. A wind chime can effectively be hung in the Partnership area of a room or a space to "call in" a partner. When angling a bed in a corner of a bedroom, a wind-chime in the corner will keep it from being dead or stagnant.

Windows—As the "eyes" of the space, they need to be kept clean and repaired. Whenever there's a question around clarity of an issue, washing the windows is an appropriate action to take to get a clear vision. They are also representative of the voice of the children who live in the space. If windows don't operate smoothly or are cracked or boarded up, the children who live there may not be heard. The correct ratio of windows to doors in a room is three to one. If there are more windows than the ratio suggests, the children may be in control. If there are more doors than the ratio suggests, the children again may not be heard.

The greatest gift a student can receive from their teacher is their blessing for the work that they're doing following in the footsteps of the teacher. As a student of Professor Thomas Lin Yun, I requested his blessing of this book. In typical fashion, he generously forwarded to me the following, done by his own hand. It is with great honor that I share these with the reader so everyone can benefit from his benedictions. The words are Professor Lin Yun's, translated from Chinese by Mary R. Hsu.

Figure I

(from right to left)

Right: Written while chanting infinite numbers of mantras on the day of the Mid-Autumn Festival, Year 2000, to bestow blessing upon benevolent persons with good karma and the readers of Carole Hyder's new masterpiece which benefits the world.

Center: Calligraphy, "Opening this book will bring great benefits."

Left: Composed by the Master of *Yun Shi Jing She,* Lin Yun, while a visitor at the study of disciple Crystal Chu in Berkeley, California.

*Note: *Yun Shi Jing She* is the name of Grandmaster Professor Lin Yun's shrines and sanctuaries all over the world.

CAROLE HYDER

Figure 1

Calligraphy by Professor Thomas Lin Yun

Figure 2

(from top to bottom)

Top: Calligraphy of the Chinese character "Tao." In smaller script is the definition of Tao according to Black Sect Tantric Buddhism: A Yin and a Yang combine as one, thereby following the laws of nature and set in motion continuously. Also in small script is the "Six-Syllable Mantra: Om Ma Ni Pad Me Hum." Written by Lin Yun while chanting mantras.

Center: Symbol of the *Yin-Yang*, with smaller symbols of the *Yin-Yang* contained within. According to Grandmaster Professor Lin Yun, there is *Yin* in *Yang*, and there is *Yang* in *Yin*. Within the *Yang* that is in *Yin*, there is another set of *Yin-Yang*, and the same within the *Yin* that is in *Yang*, and so on.

Bottom right: There is *Yang* in *Yin*, and there is *Yin* in *Yang*. When *Yin* and *Yang* are in harmony, then there will be world peace. Composed by the Master of *"Yun Shr Hsuan,"* Lin Yun, while a visitor at the study of disciple Chun-Hui Yu.

Bottom left: Written while chanting infinite numbers of mantras on the day of the Mid-Autumn Festival in the Year 2000. To bestow blessing and wisdom upon the readers, author, and publisher of Carole Hyder's new masterpiece.

道

陰一陽二者合而為一狻

CAROLE
HYDER

陰中有陽　陽中有陰

陰陽和諧　世界和平

Figure 2

Calligraphy by Professor Thomas Lin Yun

Figure 3 (from right to left)

Right: Written on the day of the Mid-Autumn Festival in the Year 2000 after offering incense and chanting mantras, to bestow blessing upon the readers, author, and publisher of Carole Hyder's new masterpiece. May they and their family members receive happiness, wealth, good health, and peace.

Center: Talisman (from top to bottom):

"The Divine order by the highest Taoist deity to immediately offer protection."

"The Five Thunder Protectors Mantra"

"The Eight Trigrams, or the *Bagua*"

"The Six-Syllable Mantra: Om Ma Ni Pad Me Hum"

"Tracing of the Nine Star Path"

In the right circles: This Talisman will offer protection to the home of a person with auspicious karma.

In the left circles: Wealth will arrive at the home of a benevolent and kind person.

Left: Composed by the Master of *Yun Shi Jin She,* Lin Yun, while a visitor at the study of disciple Crystal Chu.

*Note: *Yun Shi Jing She* is the name of Grandmaster Professor Lin Yun's shrines and sanctuaries all over the world.

Figure 3

Calligraphy by Professor Thomas Lin Yun

Figure 4

(from top to bottom)

Top: A Hidden Title Poem. In Chinese, the first characters of each line, read horizontally from right to left, says, "Feng Shui and Nature, when Harmonious, is the Best."

Tigers appear in wind

Dragons emerge from clouds

These images seem real yet untrue

Water is clear, and trees are lush

From this we can sense vital energy

Freedom and ease fill the heaven and earth

Whether this is true or not

After we have analyzed it, we will obtain new knowledge

Peace and warfare are spread equally throughout the world

Just as humor and seriousness also fill the entire universe

The ultimate is when karma begins and karma ceases

So it is best to spread this teaching to all who would like to know.

風虎雲龍假亦真
水清樹茂見精神
自由自在充天地
然否否然格物新
和戰平分全世界
諧莊佈滿大乾坤
最是緣生緣滅處
好將大道告知音

風水

CAROLE HYDER

宏著讀者作者出版者

庚辰中秋 詩贈

從龍山人林雲 時客方圓
女弟樂陶居

Figure 4

Calligraphy by Professor Thomas Lin Yun

Figure 4 *(continued)*

Bottom right: Written on the day of the Mid-Autumn Festival in the Year 2000 to be presented to the readers, author, and publisher of Carole Hyder's new masterpiece.

Bottom center: Calligraphy, "Feng Shui."

Bottom left: Composed by Lin Yun, the "Recluse Scholar Who Emerges with the Dragon," while a visitor at the study of disciple Belle Tao.

*Note: In the Chinese tradition, it is very common for scholars to have many names or aliases. In ancient Chinese folklore, tigers and dragons are regarded as mystical creatures so that when they appear, it was always with some form of natural phenomenon such as whirling winds or puffs of clouds, respectively. Since the word "Yun" in Grandmaster Professor Lin Yun's name means "cloud," he has chosen the "Recluse Scholar that Emerges with the Dragon (Tsong Long Shan Ren)" as one of his numerous scholarly names.

Figure 5

(from right to left)

Right: Written with cinnabar while adding the Three Secret Reinforcements, on the day of the Mid-Autumn Festival in the Year 2000. An old poetic work is written here to be shared with the readers of Carole Hyder's new masterpiece which brings great benefits to the world.

Top center: Calligraphy, "Three Secret Reinforcements."

Bottom center: Poem

> If you want your secret cures to be effective
>
> First of all you have got to have faith
>
> If your visualization lacks respect and piety
>
> You'll come up empty even with the Three Secret Reinforcements.

Left: Composed by Lin Yun of Black Sect Tantric Buddhism's First Temple, the Yun Lin Temple, while a visitor at the study of disciple Lynn Ho To.

Figure 5

Calligraphy by Professor Thomas Lin Yun

Figure 6

(from right to left)

Right: Written with cinnabar while chanting the highest order mantras, on the day of the Mid-Autumn Festival in the Year of the Golden Dragon, 2000. An old poetic work is written here to be shared with the readers of Carole Hyder's new masterpiece which brings great benefits to the world.

Top center: Calligraphy, "Enlightenment."

Bottom center: Poem

> Who is the winner, and who shall lose?
>
> Even the smart one is eventually confused.
>
> My advice to you is to read between the lines,
>
> And ponder the wonders of the hidden meanings.

Left: Composed by Lin Yun of Black Sect Tantric Buddhism's Second Temple, the Lin Yun Monastery, while a visitor at the study of disciple Robert Chiu.

Figure 6

Calligraphy by Professor Thomas Lin Yun

The stories never end even though, at this moment, the book does. I believe we learn from stories and from watching other people. All of these personal chronicles, or parts of them, could be any one of us. We are all working to reach our fullest potential and looking to find ways to ease through difficulties.

It is my hope that you will find some piece or two to take away for implementation in your own life. Perhaps one of the situations reminded you of your particular story. Trying even the smallest adjustment in Feng Shui can bring about some awesome shifts. I trust that in my telling these stories, you can see how to create your own experience of living Feng Shui.

Carole J. Hyder
901 W. Minnehaha Parkway
Minneapolis, MN 55419
612-823-5093
www.carolehyder.com

Carole J. Hyder was introduced to Feng Shui in 1992 after having owned a successful glass design company for over twenty years. She has presented hundreds of workshops, seminars, and keynotes on the beauty and power of Feng Shui. Carole now offers a two-year training program in Minnesota for those interested in further pursuing Feng Shui.

BOOKS BY THE CROSSING PRESS

Feng Shui Demystified

by Clear Englebert

A concise guide to the ancient principles of Feng Shui for the home, office, and garden. Author Clear Englebert explains the differences in Feng Shui variations and then discusses how to put the art into practice. This book enables anyone to practice Feng Shui for a more peaceful and harmonious home environment. It also includes a separate full-color bagua, one of Feng Shui's most powerful tools.

$10.95 • Paper • ISBN 1-58091-078-5

Wind and Water: Your Personal Feng Shui Journey

by Carol J. Hyder

This book presents Feng Shui as simple suggestions that can be done on a daily basis—each page will provide information and a corresponding activity. Instead of reading about Feng Shui, this book will provide an immediate experience of Feng Shui.

$19.95 • Paper • ISBN 1-58091-050-5

To receive a current catalog from The Crossing Press
please call toll-free, 800-777-1048.
Visit our Web site: www.crossingpress.com